FLOAT-FISHING
STRATEGIES

0 11557 00747 3

FLOAT-FISHING STRATEGIES

Tactics and techniques for drift boats,
rafts, and pontoon boats

Neale Streeks
Illustrations by Dave Hall

HEADWATER
BOOKS

STACKPOLE
BOOKS

Published by
STACKPOLE BOOKS
5067 Ritter Road
Mechanicsburg, PA 17055
www.stackpolebooks.com

Printed in the United States of America

Second edition

10 9 8 7 6 5 4 3 2 1

Library of Congress Cataloging-in-Publication Data

Streeks, E. Neale.
 Float-fishing strategies : tactics and techniques for drift boats, rafts, and pontoon boats / Neale Streeks ; illustrations by Dave Hall. — 2nd ed.
   p. cm.
 Includes index.
 ISBN-13: 978-0-8117-0747-3 (pbk.)
 ISBN-10: 0-8117-0747-4 (pbk.)
 1. Drift boats. 2. Rafts. 3. Boats and boating. 4. Fly fishing. I. Title.

SH455.4.S87 2011
799.12'2—dc22
                                                    2010031256

Contents

Introduction

Float-fishing a river is one of life's great pleasures. There is a special charm in pushing off into clear currents and watching spectacular landscapes sweep by. The sound of water lapping on the hull and scents of clean air, earth, forest, and stream are intoxicating. There are pine and cottonwood groves to float through, massive mountain ranges to lead the way, drinking wildlife to quietly observe, and clouds dressed in warm sunset pastels racing across the big western sky. Sun and breeze burnish your skin. Your whole being comes vibrantly alive. It's easy to become a river addict!

Fly-fishing for trout expands the experience, for now you must understand the water's character, fish behavior, insect hatches, and other phenomena of the river world. There are the mechanical aspects of rowing to learn and master, plus the accumulation of knowledge about river life and gamefish. All aspects of a river valley come into play in your pursuit of quarry.

Fly-fishing from drift boats and other watercraft has boomed in popularity over the last thirty years. Many who take up the sport use a hit-and-miss approach. Once they obtain the

The scenery alone is worth the trip for many fishermen, as trout usually live in beautiful places.

craft (which can be quite expensive these days), they spend no effort in learning much about its use; they figure they'll just float the river, taking it as it comes. It's common to see novice floaters bouncing off boulders, spinning out of control, and careening like pinballs down more challenging runs. Not only does this endanger those in the boat and ruin fishing opportunities, it often violates the rights of other river users. A lack of courtesy and competence on the part of many float fishers has been an unfortunate part of float fishing's continuing growth. In addition, numerous floaters drown every year, mostly novices who lack knowledge of moving water and its powerful, unforgiving qualities. Boats are lost or ruined, too—substantial investments down the drain.

When fly-fishing from an oar-powered craft, whether a raft, drift boat, pram, or pontoon boat, fly fishers have to change their fishing techniques to fully capitalize on the new opportunities that come their way. As a full-time fly-fishing guide, I get to see how many fly fishers who go on guided trips fail to recognize this fact. They must learn new approaches that are different from those most wade fishers rely on. These new approaches aren't difficult—in fact, they're easy—but unless fly fishers adopt them, they won't be as successful as they can be. A novice rower floating (or bouncing) down a river with a fly fisher, neither of whom understand float fishing's special demands, is likely to be a poor fishing team indeed.

This book covers the basic mechanics of rowing, reading rivers, and fishing, and it provides information on how to select and rig boats for a variety of fishing scenarios. Not all boats are suited for all rivers. Whitewater rivers have different demands than more placid ones that get a lot of wind. And some rivers offer multiday float-fishing adventures with streamside camping along the way. These are among the world's most beautiful float trips. We'll look at the equipment and skills needed for these, too.

It's been my goal to touch on every aspect of river float fishing that a novice would need to understand, information gleaned from thirty-plus years as a river guide. I hope to cover it in enough detail that intermediate-level floaters will get a lot out of it as well. Once these skills become second nature, your enjoyment of rivers will increase all the more.

When anglers try to fish from a drift boat, the rower's knowledge and skill can count most in the making of a great day. Not only will he get his party to its destination safely and on time, but also he will have maximized the fishing potential by slowing down the craft as it floats through the best fishing spots.

Safety is paramount, of course. Floating rivers involves risks—dangers that seem to arise so quickly that any hesitation in decision making and reaction can be injurious to life and property and even fatal. Human nature often leads the unlearned and inexperienced to do the exact opposite of what should be done, facilitating disaster instead of averting it. River knowledge doesn't come naturally; it has to be learned.

The object of this book, then, is to provide a solid base of information for novices to intermediate-level float fishers, a base that will help them understand moving water, use the proper rowing skills to avert danger, and provide ideas to help catch more fish with nymphs, dry flies, and streamers. It's a lot easier to absorb the float-fishing skills this book provides than it is to spend years in hit-and-miss experimentation trying to figure them out.

Even those who don't fish might enjoy learning more about rowing and river life. The more you understand the infinite intricacies of water and stone, algae and aspen, insect, fish, mammal, and bird, the more lasting enjoyment you may reap. There is little that can match the beauty and richness of natural rivers in uncompromised settings. The ripples, eddies, and glides of moving water and the rings of rising trout and banter

The final objective, a fine brown trout. For some types of fishing, such as hitting the banks with streamers, floating is the way to go.

of migrating waterfowl have a hypnotizing effect and an undeniable appeal to the human psyche, which otherwise seems to get lost in modern society. The feel of oars in your hands, the push of clean flowing water, and the sight of wild landscapes sweeping by all enrich life. The effects are immediate and gratifying. Views from the river are always interesting.

1

Basic Rowing Skills

Rowing is a fairly basic physical action, yet there are subtleties to consider. Oars can be mechanically fixed at the oarlocks or spin free for ultimate hand control. There's the lazy pace of slow, open water and the vigorous demands and split-second decision making of tough whitewater. As with most sports, rowing becomes an art in its extreme applications. Because our purpose is primarily fishing, the emphasis is on smooth control to maximize the angler's casting advantage. You don't usually need a power stroke, but one that incorporates finesse with good timing.

The simple act of lifting the oar blades out of the water, pushing the handles forward (which, with the use of the oarlocks as fulcrums, swings the blades back upstream), dipping the blades in the water, and then pulling smoothly on the handles until you're leaning backward is a rhythmic and relaxing routine. A few facets of this basic rowing stroke warrant closer inspection. We'll look at them one step at a time.

Place your hands over the oar handles in a natural fashion so that you are looking at the backs of your hands. You can put your thumbs over the ends of the oar handles or wrap them

OAR-BLADE ANGLES IN THE WATER

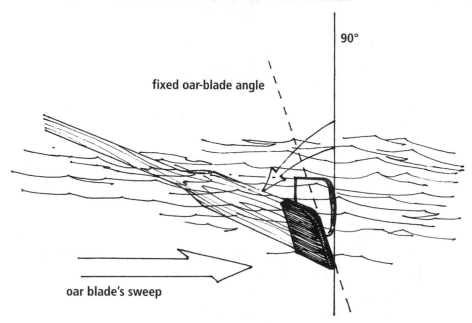

When an oar is fixed in position (with an Oar Right, pin and clip, or by hand), the top of the blade should be tilted back slightly toward the stern. As your power stroke finishes and lifts toward the surface, this angle gives the best bite.

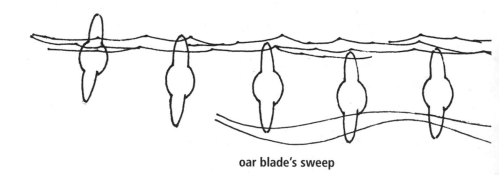

oar blade's sweep

underneath. When using a horn oarlock with a traditional stopper on your oar, you'll have to keep the oar blades at the proper angle by using a firm grip and continually adjusting them as they rotate slightly through the course of the oar stroke. Drawing the oar blade through the water and occasionally hitting the bottom tends to rotate it in your hands. The angle of the oar blade has to do with the direction you're pushing the water during the strongest part of the stroke. It changes slightly as the oar stroke progresses from beginning to end. The blade angle can be rolled or changed to do other things, too, such as feathering, to brake gently, and ruddering and sweeping while pointed toward the bow. (We'll examine these techniques later.)

In any case, your grip on the oar must be firm enough to maintain the correct blade angle. You'll know you're way off if you make a power stroke and almost fall backward off your seat! This happens when the blades are accidentally spun to a horizontal position that is parallel with the river's surface. There will be no water resistance, and because you're used to leaning on the oars for support when they're held at the proper angle during an oar stroke, you will fall back.

Routinely glance at your oar blades to see if they're at the proper angle. With a lot of experience, you can tell what the

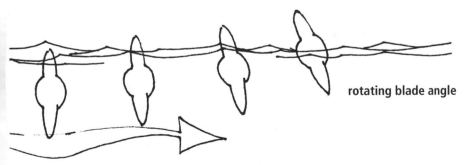

rotating blade angle

Horn oar locks allow experienced rowers to rotate the blade angle slightly through the course of an oar stroke. This gives maximum efficiency to each pull. It becomes automatic, done mostly by feel.

oar-blade angle is by feel alone. You might even rotate the angle a bit with your wrists during the oar stroke to gain the best pushing angle throughout the oar's path.

When lifting the oars out of the water in preparation for the next oar stroke, raise the blades no more than a few inches above the water's surface. Any more is a waste of energy. You might have to lift them higher in rapids and waves to clear the turbulence. You might also have to raise them up to pass over boulders or logs protruding from the river. Beginners tend to lift oars too far out of the water, splash them back down, and then pull them through the water too deeply.

After you have swung the oar blades back upstream, dip them quietly in the water to prepare for the back-rowing pull. Don't splash your oars down into the water. Remember that you're trying to sneak up on trout, which are wild animals in a wild setting.

The oar blades should be just barely underwater. Digging them deeply decreases your leverage since they are more likely to hit the bottom and will be harder to lift back up. In turbulent water, whirling subsurface currents can get such a grip on deep oars that you can barely get them back up and out of the water. This momentarily handicaps rowing, sometimes in critical situations. Keep oar strokes relatively shallow, smooth, and quiet.

Immediately after dipping the oar blades in the water, begin pulling back and leaning into them. Rowing anglers usually calls for an easy but continuous pace. Slowing the boat down is every bit as important as positioning it advantageously when it comes to good fishing. It's all very rhythmic, with pauses occasionally taken, and only in slow-water, nonmaneuvering situations.

When pulling back on the oars, maximize your leverage by keeping the blades just barely under the surface. You might have to observe them when learning to get the feel for the right depth, to make sure you have the blade angled correctly with a

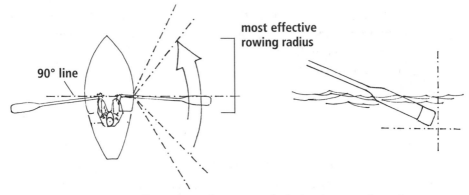

90° line

most effective rowing radius

The most energy-efficient part of an oar stroke is the short arc shown here closest to the 90-degree line outside the oarlock. Experienced rowers tend to use short oar strokes that look effortless (except in demanding situations). Beginners usually make too wide a rowing arc, which wastes energy and gains little power.

When making a backstroke, dig the oar just deep enough in the water to cover the blade. Beginners tend to dig too deeply, which dissipates leverage and oar power and can also jam the oar blade into the river bottom.

The oar-blade angle should vary from straight up and down to a slight tilt, with the top of the blade leaning back slightly toward the stern. This gives a better bite on the water as the backstroke follows through and raises the oar before it is lifted out for the next stroke.

sure grip. Don't forget to constantly look up and ahead for river hazards, though, while also working to keep anglers ideally positioned.

In addition to digging in the oars too deeply, beginners also tend to make too wide an oar sweep, covering too much of a semicircular path with the blade. This overdone oar stroke inefficiently pushes more water perpendicular to, rather than parallel to, the boat and its intended path. It's usually easier and more effective to take three shorter strokes than two overlong ones. Experienced rowers use tiny little oar strokes. The novice will tend to overrow, dig too deeply with the oars, flail them about in the air and water, and in general, use way too much energy in a less than efficient fashion. At times, you need extra power and a slightly longer oar stroke, using all the strength in your back, abdomen, legs, and arms. But practice economizing your efforts while you keep the boat in position.

Back Rowing

The first rule of rowing, whether for fishing or in whitewater, is to do all your maneuvering with backstrokes—by pulling on the oars, not by pushing on them. Arm, back, stomach, and leg muscles work together to make backstroking much more powerful than simply pushing the oars forward against the water. Most beginners want to push the oars forward, perhaps because they themselves are facing forward. It seems the natural thing to do at times. The biggest problem with this arises when novice rowers are faced with serious river hazards and think that they can row forward to get away from them. They usually can't. Indeed, rowing forward only increases the speed and rate with which you approach an obstacle, even when rowing down and across stream. The forward stroke is weak, generally making little progress across the current's flow and away from the obstruction. A common scenario is when beginners start off by trying to row forward to get away from a hazard, realize they can't, try to reposition (pivot) the boat, and finally begin back rowing, but all too late. Collisions in such cases are common.

Certainly, rowing forward is an option at times, usually when you're just trying to make time down a straight stretch of obstacle-free river. But anytime you need to avoid a hazard, immediately revert to back rowing. This slows down the craft and allows maximum lateral maneuverability (ferrying).

In fishing situations, you almost always want to be constantly back-rowing at an easy pace to slow down the boat anyway so that you can cover the water more efficiently with your

A steady back-rowing cadence gives you time to look for fish, scan the best water, and fish it thoroughly as you slowly progress downstream.

flies. Consider that the boat is often out in the faster currents, whereas you often want to place the fly in slower bank waters, eddies, and places where trout don't have to fight the full force of the current. If you do not back-row, the boat whisks by all those promising pockets. Fishers can barely manage a brief, half-good presentation. There is nothing more annoying than trying to fish from a drift boat that is traveling too fast and is not in the absolute best position for casting presentations. A rower who's going with the flow can be a serious irritation to those in the boat who wish to fish, except when deep water indicator nymphing.

It's important to keep up a steady pace, however intense, when rowing anglers. I make an oar stroke about every three seconds when guiding. I'm often rowing over eight hours a day

Once you master the basic oar strokes and learn to avoid hazards, you can focus on the finer points—keeping your casters in good position and spotting fish.

(out of more than ten on the river). This adds up to 1,200 oar strokes an hour, or 9,600 oar strokes a day. This is a common rowing pace for hardworking fishing guides. Of course, it's so habitual that it doesn't seem like that much work. If it's been a really tough rowing day (usually due to wind or high water), my legs feel it the most at the end of the day, along with the skin on the palms of my hands. If your hands aren't used to rowing, consider wearing gloves.

As you steadily and easily back-row, you are facing forward, which is downstream. Your goal is to keep the anglers in your boat at a steady distance from the target water so they can fish with a fixed length of fly line. Don't let the boat drift within 10 feet of shore and then row it out 100 feet away. When hitting the banks, keep the boat a constant 50 feet or so away, or whatever distance is easy and effective for your particular fishing party. It takes constant observation and planning to keep a boat slowed down and in the perfect fishing position, for the boat is nothing more than a platform from which to cast. If your party is float-fishing and it's your turn at the oars, it's your job to position the boat conscientiously and to slow it down. This doesn't allow much break in concentration. Again, this becomes somewhat second nature with experience but always requires some thought to maintain the proper distance from shore.

There's a lot on the water to test and distract you, too, like sideslipping currents, whirlpooling eddies, crosswinds, and rocks to be maneuvered around—not to mention beautiful scenery and wildlife to gaze at! With practice, your mind analyzes the river's flow with computerlike precision. You look to the bank every five seconds to calculate your distance from it, rhythmically continue making backstrokes, plot upcoming maneuvers around obstacles, duck low casts—all in a nonstop mental and physical flow paced to match the river's cadence. Funny thing is, all this is usually quite relaxing and fun!

Oar and Oarlock Designs

Oars and oarlock designs affect the hands' duties at the oars. Horn oarlocks with oars that have stoppers are a common arrangement on drift boats, rafts, and some pontoon boats, and I use them on my drift boat. Others prefer fixed-oar setups that help maintain the proper oar-blade position.

Horn Oarlocks, Oars with Stoppers

This is the arrangement I use on my drift boat, with epoxied rope tightly wound over a length of the oar to keep it from popping out through the horn. On the handle end of this rope-wound segment is a rubber stopper. This keeps the oars at the right length for rowing while also stopping them from sliding out through the horns and into the river when I let go of them. With this arrangement, the hands must keep the oar blades at the correct rowing angle in the river. Experienced rowers can judge the oar-blade angle by feel, but beginners should glance at the blade angle as they swing the oars back upstream for another stroke.

Though many experienced boatmen prefer oars that can be feathered and spun to meet varying situations, Oar Rights or pins and clips maintain the blade at a fixed angle, eliminating the need to constantly adjust the blade angle. Once the oar blade is locked in to a good rowing angle, you can loosen your grip and give blade angle no more immediate thought.

An *Oar Right* is a type of oar stopper that fits between the oarlock horns and keeps the oar blade vertical, so you can focus on other things. The *Convertible Oar Right* gives you the ability to adjust to an open oar lock for full feathering ability or an Oar Right.

Pins and Clips

Pins and clips are a more unusual-looking arrangement that is often used on whitewater rafts. A clip is hose-clamped onto the oar. Its specialized design allows it to be jammed onto the pin, which is attached to the rowing frame in place of a horn oarlock. This locks the oar blade firmly in at a good rowing angle that can be changed only by loosening the hose clamps on the oar and clip, rotating the oar by the blade, and retightening the hose clamps.

Oar Right oar stoppers keep the oar handles spaced properly while maintaining the angle of the oar blade in the water.

Pins and clips also allow the oar to pop free from the pin, should the oar slam into a rock or cliff wall, a situation in which it might otherwise break. (Horn oarlocks allow this, too.) This is a common occurrence in running whitewater. Originally, boatmen tied in their oars, and many still do, because once the oar clip blows off the pin, the oar can easily fall overboard. The force of impact and danger of capsizing diminish one's chances of holding on to a loose 10-foot oar in raging water.

A more recent alternative to tying in the oars are plastic oar stirrups. These lasso an oar that blows off a pin until the boatman can reposition himself at his seat and grab it again. On big-water expeditions of several days, it's wise to both tie in your oars (and all your other equipment) and use stirrups. At least one spare oar should always be taken, too.

(*continues on next page*)

Pins and clips are rarely seen on fishing boats. The less cumbersome and cheaper Oar Rights have largely taken their place on mellower trout rivers.

Setting up the Oars

Regardless of oarlock design, you must consider how closely together the oar handles are positioned when oars are measured and set up. (The stopper or pin and clip position becomes, for all practical purposes, permanent while rowing, though most can be changed.) Most people like to leave just a few inches between their oar handles when they're extended out all the way and held horizontally. If they're any closer, it's easy to pinch or crush your thumbs between them when rowing. A few boatmen actually like to overlap their oar handles and row in a circular or offset motion, with one hand going over the other, to avoid finger-crushing collisions. The idea here is that the longer the part of the oar on the rower's side of the oarlock (within reason), the more powerful the rowing leverage. This overlapping-oar technique is best left to the experienced, for occasionally smashing your fingers until you're habituated to the style is no great fun.

You'll often see boats rigged with the oars going to the opposite extreme—they are too far apart. This is often done as an oversight by novice boat owners. What happens when you fix your oars too far apart is (1) you lose leverage and (2) the weight of the oar outside the oarlock, that length of oar you pick up and swing back upstream hundreds and even thousands of times a day, is increased. Too much space between oar handles and too much oar outside the boat make for a decidedly harder rowing day. If the oar blade weighs 5 pounds and you make 5,000 oar strokes a day, you've lifted an accumulated 25,000 pounds by the end of the day!

(*continues on page 14*)

RIGGING AN OAR

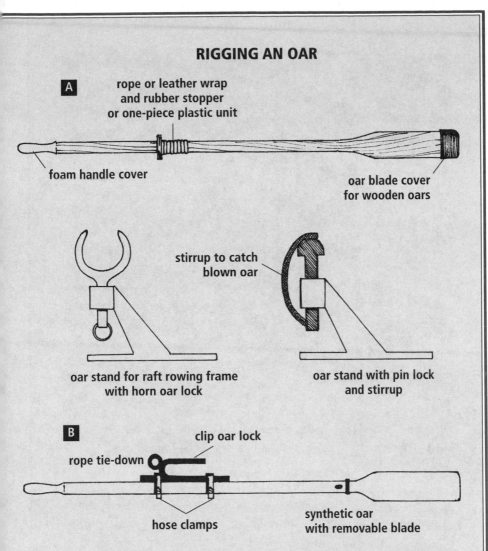

A
rope or leather wrap
and rubber stopper
or one-piece plastic unit

foam handle cover

oar blade cover
for wooden oars

stirrup to catch
blown oar

oar stand for raft rowing frame
with horn oar lock

oar stand with pin lock
and stirrup

B

clip oar lock

rope tie-down

hose clamps

synthetic oar
with removable blade

A. Traditionally rigged oars featured wraps of rope or leather to build up the thickness of the oar diameter so the oar wouldn't pop out of the horn oar lock. A rubber oar stop was then secured to keep the oar from slipping out of the horn. Proper oar-blade angle is maintained by the rower's grip.

B. Clip oar locks have been popular on big whitewater rivers. These slip over a pin. This keeps the oar blade at the proper rowing angle and allows the oar to pop free should it hit a rock under extreme water pressure.

When held parallel to the water, oar handles should be just a few inches apart from each other to give maximum oar leverage—without crushing your thumbs.

Only recently have oars with adjustable weighting systems in the oar handles hit the market (after how many millennia of rowing?). You can add or subtract weight till the oars are balanced to your liking. I have long thought that an oar should automatically balance when you let go of it, with the blade lifting itself clear of the water until its shaft comes slowly to rest at the horizontal. In that way, the amount of weight you've lifted with each oar stroke is significantly reduced by the end of the day. This is no small point when you're averaging 10,000 oar strokes a day. ■

ANTICIPATING THE RIVER

Skilled rowing is all in the planning. Decisions on boat position-ing (the angle across the current in which the stern's pointed) and backstroking effort need to be made well in advance of the hazard. Drift boats and rafts don't respond immediately to oar strokes. It takes several strokes to start building some inertia and speed. This inertia carries on a bit after you stop rowing, too. Overrowing beginners make too many oar strokes to miss an obstacle, with the resulting momentum carrying them much farther aside than they meant to go, even running them into the bank or another hazard.

If you see a boulder coming, pivot the boat until it's in a position where you can back-row away from it long before reaching it. Ferrying across the current at an angle of about 45 degrees both slows you down and allows lateral progress across the river. Remember, the back of the boat needs to point in the direction you want to go, not the front.

Most rowed boats respond rather slowly to the oars at first, so advance setup is necessary. After pivoting or setting the boat up, begin an easy backstroke to get some momentum going long before you reach your obstacle. This usually takes several strokes to begin. As you get closer to a hazard, you might need to backstroke harder. On the other hand, your first few back-strokes may have built up enough momentum and carried you far enough to the side of it to suffice. Each encounter will be a little different.

You want to miss obstacles, but not by more than necessary when fishermen are aboard. Beginners have a tendency to over-row, taking ten ferrying backstrokes to skirt an obstacle that needs only three strokes to miss. Instead of easing around a rock and missing it by 5 feet, they shoot across the river and miss it by 50. Overrowing makes fishing much more difficult. Although you're better off safe than sorry, overrowing can get beginners in trouble in boulder-studded rapids, where the way in which you shave hazards and set up for the next one can be critical. Knowing how much power you need to maneuver around objects in various situations takes experience. There are times and places when the elements will keep pushing you into the hazard you're trying to avoid, for instance, sharp, swift bends in rivers, steep water-gathering drops, crosswinds, and sideslipping currents. Here, extra effort and quick decision making are in order. On a straight stretch of even-flowing river with no wind, pivoting and backstroke ferrying can be quite leisurely.

The best thing to do is spend plenty of time at the oars under a good coach. Start out on forgiving rivers and progress to more difficult ones as your proficiency develops. To be painfully literal, don't get in over your head right from the start. There are several drownings every year on Montana rivers alone. Most occur in spring and early summer, when rivers are high with snowmelt and are ice cold. Floaters are eager to get on stream, especially the novices with new boats. New logjams may have formed since winter, and high water tends to shove boats right into obstacles at this time. Waves, holes, whirlpools, and turbulence are all bigger and faster during runoff. Unfortunately, many floaters look at a boat trip like a carnival ride— until they flip in frigid, roiling water, losing gear and risking lives. The sudden uncontrollable shock of landing in freezing water and the resulting hypothermia quickly erode responsiveness and alert thought. Panic and senseless floundering often ensue. Many river drownings involve alcohol and the absence of life jackets, let alone wet suits.

It's a good idea to row some whitewater rivers as you progress in experience, to hone your rowing and water-reading skills and to build your knowledge and confidence so that rowing becomes second nature. Decision making should become quick and comprehensive. Other people's lives and property can be in your hands.

Start rowing on easier waters under a good coach. Work your way up to more challenging rivers as your rowing skills become second nature. Beginners often underestimate a river's power and potential for disaster.

BASIC MANEUVERING

As I keep emphasizing, all of your maneuvering should be done with backstrokes. The next habit to develop is pointing the stern (rear) of the boat in the direction you want to go. This is achieved through oar manipulation. We'll call it "pivoting." After the boat is pivoted, with the stern pointed in the direction you want to go, pull back on both oars, propelling the craft back and at a 45-degree angle to the current. Let's step back a bit to go through these maneuvers one at a time and look at each more closely.

Launch sites can be easy or demanding. Some have ramps; others require that you carry the boat some distance. What's just downstream might be placid or immediately challenging.

Putting In and Pushing Off

Most put-ins are easy enough to negotiate, but in difficult pieces of water, even pushing off from the bank to start your float can be tricky. The current might immediately push you into a logjam or rock garden.

Most put-ins or launch sites won't present a problem, but in some instances you need immediate control, and a novice won't have much, if any, time to figure out much about the rowing game. One common situation calling for immediate launch control is when floaters stop to scout a rapid, logjam, or other hazard before floating by it. There can be just one good entry slot or chute leading into a rapid. The boat not only needs to be in that spot but also might need to be set up properly as it goes down the chute in order to begin the next boulder-dodging maneuver. Rapids wait for no one!

There are still other situations where the boat not only needs to be in the right spot, with the stern pointed the right way, but also needs to have some inertia built up through back rowing if it's going to miss the next quickly approaching hazard. Entry position, setup or ferrying angle, and preestablished momentum can all be absolutely necessary in tight rowing situations. After scouting a rapid, the need for a good push-off and launch facilitating immediate control can be critical. In serious situations, such entries need to be discussed so that everybody clearly understands what to do and when to do it.

The trick here is to get the boat's stern pointed in the right direction from the very start: upstream and at a 30- to 45-degree angle to the current. This is best achieved by having the boat "parallel parked" along the bank for starters. We'll presume the boat has a rower and two fishermen. The boat is held in place, but floating (not half hung up on the bank), by the angling team. The rower gets in first so as to be instantly ready to row when the moment of truth comes.

The next steps in critical situations will require good timing, because a strong current can easily spin the boat out of control. The stern angler now pushes his end out at about a 30- to 45-degree angle across the current. This should put the boat at a good angle to ferry out to midstream and clear the oar from the bank so the rower will be able to get an immediate dig in the water. The stern angler quickly jumps in the boat, gets a good grip on something, and sits down.

Just moments after the stern angler pushes off, the bow angler pushes the front of the boat straight back while it's still at the 30- to 45-degree ferrying angle to the current and jumps in. If he waits too long to push off, the current will have swung the stern of the boat downstream, and if an immediate maneuver was needed to pull away from a hazard, the rower will be in a bad position to deal with it. It will take extra time and distance to spin the boat back to a good ferrying angle, especially

PULLING AWAY FROM THE BANK

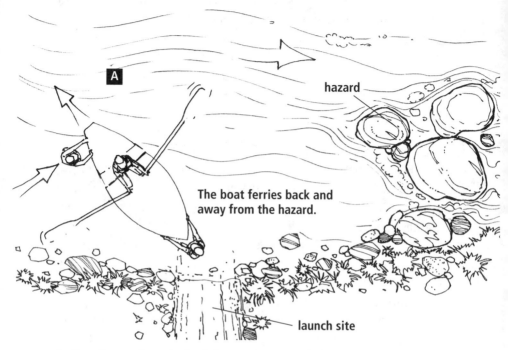

hazard

The boat ferries back and away from the hazard.

launch site

A. To pull away from the bank in complete control, the stern angler pushes the stern out to a near 45-degree ferrying angle and jumps in. The bow angler then pushes the boat straight back and gets in. The rower now pulls hard on both oars. He may need extra power on the midstream oar to keep the stern from swinging downstream.

if it's been spun all the way around and is now facing downstream rather than up. The bankside oar can also be inhibited by shallow water or the bank itself, because the current will most likely push the boat back toward shore.

The boat type has some bearing here. Rafts and prams have lower bows (front ends) and are generally easier to jump into after pushing off. Drift boats have high front ends and can be difficult to scale, especially for older and less athletic fisher-

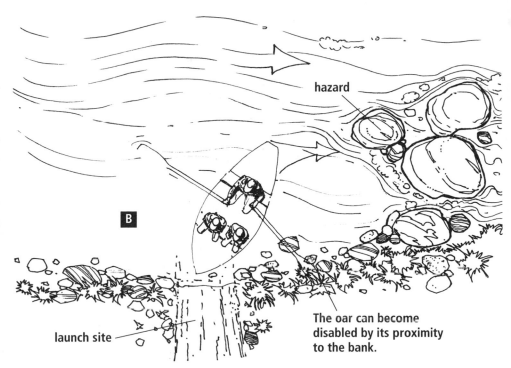

hazard

B

The oar can become
disabled by its proximity
to the bank.

launch site

B. A bad push-off can result in the stern swinging downstream in a strong
current. The rower can get into a difficult position and have a hard time
pulling away from the impending hazard.

men. In this case, it's best for the bow and stern anglers to get
in first, and then the rower should push the boat out at the
proper angle and quickly jump in. Most drift boats have anchor
systems, too, which allow everyone to get in the boat and get
seated before the boatman angles the craft out across the currents. The boat is anchored parallel to the shoreline. The rower
pulls up the anchor, takes a couple of quick strokes with the oar
to angle the stern out 30 degrees into the current, and then
backstrokes with both oars, ferrying out into the river.

When the oarsman is pushing out without an anchor system, he will also have to deal with the oars. These are usually in the locks and either trailing downstream in the water or pulled across and resting upon the gunwales (upper sides of the boat). In either case, he'll have to jump over or climb around the oars while getting to his seat. This, too, requires at least a little thought in critical situations.

Personal pontoon craft are light, agile, and easily pivoted. As with larger boats, angle the stern at a 30- to 45-degree angle upstream, and back ferry out into the river. Plot your evasive maneuvers and carry them out in advance.

A last hazard to avoid when launching is other people's boats. There are some beautiful new wooden and shiny fiberglass boats on the river these days. Their owners can get hot when some unskilled or mindless floater slams into the side of their craft, putting a big scar in it. A ding in some types of fine craft could cost hundreds of dollars to repair. If you're a novice and have the choice, try launching downstream of other boats so you have open water to get established in.

Pivoting

A boat is pivoted in one of two ways. You can leave one oar in place in the water, which acts as a brake on that side, and then take several backstrokes with the other oar. This will swing the stern around at an easy pace until it's pointed in the direction you want to go. It usually takes just a few strokes to pivot or turn a boat unless it's particularly heavy or you're in very turbulent water.

The second way to pivot is by pulling back with one oar and pushing forward with the other oar, rather than planting it as a brake. This speeds up the pivoting process, which can be important in some serious rock- or log-choked stretches of river, where quick decision making and instant action are called for.

PIVOTING THE BOAT

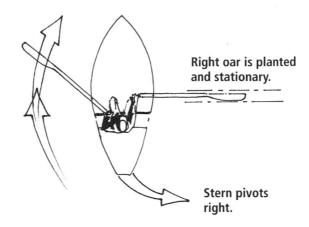

A

Backstroke several times with the left oar.

A backstroke is made by lifting the oar blade out of the water, pushing the handle forward, and then dipping the blade and pulling backward.

Right oar is planted and stationary.

Stern pivots right.

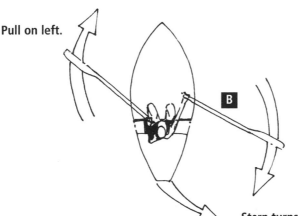

Pull on left.

A forward stroke is made by lifting the oar blade out of the water, pulling the handle backward, and then dipping it and pushing it forward.

B

Push on right.

Stern turns more quickly to the right.

A. There are two common ways of pivoting, or turning. The first method uses only one oar for power. The right one, in this case, is planted as a brake that holds that side still while the left side pivots.

B. The second and faster method of turning is the push-pull pivot. In this case, the left oar is pulled through the water and the right oar is pushed. This speedier way of pivoting takes a little practice to master and tends to confuse rowers at first.

From a fishing point of view, a quick and sudden pivot is undesirable. A standing angler can be knocked over by vigorous pivoting, especially if it's unannounced. Indeed, when I row anglers, I often tell them in advance when I'm going to pivot or pull back extra hard on the oars, because either can cause standing anglers to fall down, even if they are in knee braces. What you want when rowing anglers is a very smooth and polished rowing cadence that does not disrupt the fishing. Ideally, passengers should hardly feel your rowing strokes as you keep them in the best possible fishing position. Heavy water and river hazards can require vigorous rowing, though, and passengers should be alerted to your course of action so they can secure themselves. It's not that rare for a rower to actually dump a stern angler right into the river on an abrupt pivot or stronger-than-average oar stroke. Communication is key.

The push-pull pivot takes practice to become instinctual. Most beginners have a little trouble remembering which oar to do what with for a while. The best thing to do is get out on a mellow river and pivot, ferry, and pivot again like crazy. Do it dozens of times, until it starts coming naturally. You don't want to draw a mental blank when you suddenly find yourself in a tricky spot.

Ferrying
This is a common term for crossing a river. By rowing at roughly a 45-degree angle upstream with your stern leading the way, you can cross a river without being swept too far downstream. In mellow flows, you can actually row upstream against the current and cross to the other side.

With your boat at a 45-degree angle, the current coming downstream will deflect off the craft's side, helping to push it in the intended direction. In contrast, if you row a boat completely sideways to the current, the full force of the current will grab the craft and push it downstream, perhaps farther than you want to go.

FERRYING

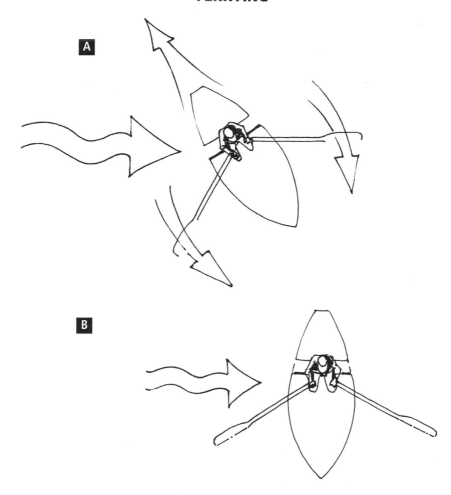

A. The boatman rows at a 30- to 45-degree upstream angle to the current to cross a river. The current deflects of the upstream side of the boat, helping to push it in the right direction while still sliding under the stern. This allows the boat to cross without being swept too far downstream. Note that river currents don't always flow parallel to the banks.

B. If a boat is angled too straight across the river, it will suddenly be shoved downstream at a more rapid rate, at actual current speed. This could mean zipping by some valuable fishing water on the other side!

If you pull out and cross a river directly sideways to the current, strong currents and waves can easily flip boats. You should enter a very strong current at less than a 45-degree angle, more like a 30-degree angle. It's the moment you first enter a rushing current that presents the problem. This generally occurs when you pull away from the bank during a launch or when you pull out of midriver eddies (such as from downstream of boulders, bridge pilings, or islands). A sideways entry puts the almost stationary boat immediately out into a rushing torrent in extreme cases. The water will pile up against the upstream side of the boat and tend to climb up over the gunwale and shove it under. The end result can be an alarmingly fast and disconcerting flip. It happens quite frequently to beginners on powerful rivers, most often when they are high with snowmelt and deadly cold. Low-sided craft, including canoes, prams, and small rafts, flip easiest, but even big rafts and drift boats go over every year.

When a boat enters a strong current at a 15- to 45-degree back-ferrying angle, the water pushes against or slides under the stern, which is much less likely to flip it. This is why modern rafts, drift boats, and prams have upturned bows and sterns (called "rocker") to allow the current to slide under the boat and push it up rather than under. Flat-bottomed boats and canoes (those without any rocker) are much more likely to be rolled and flipped under similar conditions and are harder to navigate where constant maneuvering is required, even when rowed by competent hands.

Think about what water will do to your craft and where it will be carried before you enter strong or dangerous flows. Be prepared to row strongly, make fast decisions, and do some quick powerhouse pivot turns. In these more extreme cases, passengers should be seated, wearing life jackets, and holding on. They might even want to have an extra paddle on hand to help with any last-second maneuvering. Again, we're talking

ROCKER

rocker

Drift boats, prams, rafts, and well-designed personal watercraft have appreciable rocker, or end-to-end curvature, to allow for quick pivots and maneuverability. It also allows strong currents to run under the hull, rather than pushing against the stern. (Rocker and high sides also make them windblown!)

Lake canoes and other craft without rocker are more difficult to maneuver in tight spots and thus more prone to flipping.

about extreme cases here, but those are just the ones you want to understand and train yourself for. Rivers can be unforgiving.

Once you're safely out in the current, ferrying over to wher ever it is you want to go, things should be a little easier because you're now traveling closer to, but slower than, river speed. Some basic maneuvering will soon come in to play. You will need to assess and row around rocks, logs, bridge abutments, gravel bars, and the like. At the same time, you'll be slowing down the craft, putting anglers in the best position for fishing.

Since it takes several oar strokes before a boat starts building up much ferrying momentum, preplanning your pivot turns and ferrying maneuvers is necessary. The boat will also continue the side-ferrying momentum for a while after you stop rowing. With practice, you'll get used to the momentum; it's important for navigating the boat properly.

Another concern in ferrying is the depth of the river. You want to be continually shifting your field of vision to include all your rowing contingencies. This includes more than figuring your rowing route and how far you are from the good fishing

PULLING OUT INTO STRONG CURRENTS

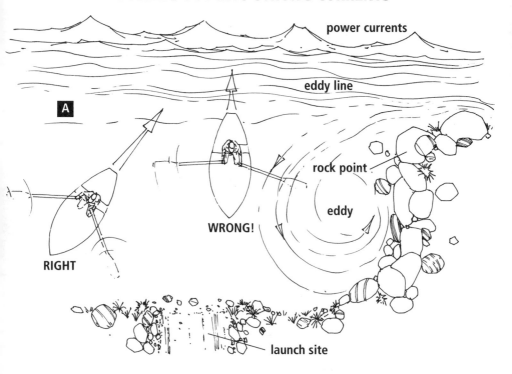

water; you also need to be alert to the depth of the water in which you're about to stick your oar. You might remember our earlier discussion about not digging the oar blade too deeply in the water. This is especially important when you're somewhat or completely sideways to the current, for then your downstream oar could potentially jam blade-first into the streambed. Boulders or logs might be jutting up toward the surface, or the river might be shallow near the banks. In any case, you need to be aware of river depth and pay particular attention to the downstream oar's field of play. Jamming the downstream oar into the bottom during a ferry will wake you right up. The oar blade can break, or it can wedge between rocks. In heavier currents, the boat might wheel out of control while you reset the

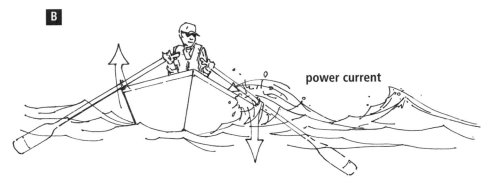

power current

A. When pulling out into a strong current, drop downstream a bit from eddy zones of great current-speed contrast. Keep a sharp 30-degree or so ferrying angle to the current when first entering it so that the swift water slides under your stern.

B. If you pull out into a powerful current from an eddy with your boat sideways to the current, water will tend to heave up and possibly over the upstream side. In extreme cases, this can shove the upstream side of your boat under the water, rolling and flipping it. This is a frequent occurrence with novice rowers, especially in low-sided craft.

oar, which has probably been blown from its oarlock. Low-sided craft might flip if a downstream oar is jammed in a swift current, for the boat is brought to a sudden stop and water begins climbing the upstream side. A downstream oar can also be knocked loose from the rower's grip if it jams into the streambed. Lost oars are common occurrences in these situations, unless you have the foresight to either tie the oars in beforehand or use oar stirrups.

Another type of ferrying challenge happens often on big western rivers, where the wind can really whip. A downstream gale will start blowing the drift boat downstream at a much faster rate than the current if the oarsman lets it get out of control. And because drift boats have a lot of rocker, or an

COMMON MISHAPS WHEN BOAT
IS SIDEWAYS TO CURRENT

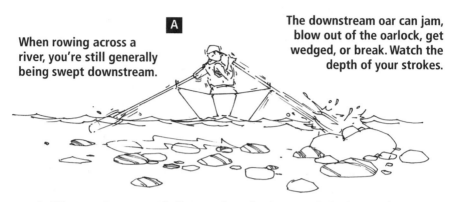

When rowing across a river, you're still generally being swept downstream.

The downstream oar can jam, blow out of the oarlock, get wedged, or break. Watch the depth of your strokes.

A. When rowing across shallow reaches of a river, watch the bottom for depth and how deeply you dig your downstream oar. It's common to jam the downstream oar blade into the river bottom, which can give the boat a serious jolt and sudden canter. It can also break or wedge oar blades on the bottom and pop oars from their locks. This has the potential to ruin your setup when entering a challenging bit of water. Another common occurrence is when an oar hits the river bottom, blows out of the lock, and jams the oar handle into your side or face. This has happened to me more than once and can really hurt.

upturned hull fore and aft, they blow like leaves and consequently are pushed sideways to the current. When the rower of a side-blown drift boat dips his downstream oar in the river (especially after not rowing for a while and letting the boat's downstream speed greatly exceed the current speed), that downstream oar can act like a sudden brake. This problem is usually limited to boats with horn oarlocks, where the rower's grip must maintain the oar-blade angle. If the blade gets turned sideways a little, the boat's windblown momentum shoves the oar down deeper, where its steep angle brakes the boat to a sudden stop. The boat will lurch over, being partly pulled under

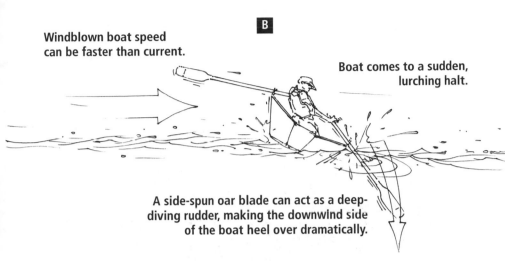

Windblown boat speed
can be faster than current.

Boat comes to a sudden,
lurching halt.

A side-spun oar blade can act as a deep-
diving rudder, making the downwind side
of the boat heel over dramatically.

B. When a downriver wind is howling, your boat can be going faster than
the current. If you stop rowing, the boat will blow sideways. Beginning
rowers tend to get fatigued and take a rest, and then start back up as
they approach a hazard. Should the downstream oar blade be planted
horizontally rather than vertically, it will dig deep, causing its side of the
boat to suddenly halt, dive, and lurch. I've been in situations where this
almost flipped the boat.

on the downstream side by the oar's diving impetus and partly
pushed up on the upstream side by the wind. The sudden jolt
of the oar's braking action can even throw everybody out of
their seats and to the downstream side. This makes that side,
which is already diving a bit, go down even farther. Flips in
such cases are not out of the question. I was in a couple of
these incidents a few years back on the wide Missouri, with a
novice at the oars. It wasn't that he was a complete novice, just
a novice at rowing in 40 to 60 mph winds, something a guide
has to face every few days.

Most of your ferrying experiences will be of the easy and
enjoyable sort, an exuberant oneness with your boat. Do, how-

Once rowing skills become second nature, you can become a trout hunter.

ever, note how these factors affect your rowing. Become aware of your limitations as well as those of your boat in more intense encounters.

Once rowing skills become habitual and second nature to you, you'll be able to concentrate more on the fishing possibilities. This will take time spent on the river, but when you find you don't have to think about the rowing much anymore, you'll be well on your way. You'll start noticing subtler rising fish, trouty seams you may never have seen before, and the shape of fish under clear water. You can now be the trout hunter, with little to distract you from that focus.

Before going on to a discussion of river hazards and fishing skills, though, I want to introduce you to a rowing method that's largely unknown to most floaters. Fishing guides who have discovered it use it extensively. It allows the best fine-tuned positioning, keeping anglers in the best casting positions more of the time, with less pivoting to bother the stern angler. We call it the crawl stroke. It's the focus of Chapter 2.

2

The Crawl Stroke

Years of rowing on smaller rivers with lots of rocks to dodge inspired me and other guides to perfect some variant rowing skills. These differ from whitewater skills somewhat, because forceful water, turbulence, and waves are rarely part of our float-fishing game. It's a subtlety of oar strokes that counts in fishing, rowing to keep anglers in the best possible position while slowing the craft to a standstill—all done so smoothly that passengers hardly know you're rowing. The boat and anglers aren't jerked around by unnecessary or violent pivots. One strategy, for example, is to go over shallow rocks with a raft, high-centering them rather than rowing around them. The raft floor stretches up and over rounded shallow or even protruding rocks quite easily. At low water, it's a nonstop rock-dodging game. High-centering some rocks allows you to keep a straighter rowing track down the river and to avoid pivot maneuvers whenever possible. This improves the anglers' position in the river in relation to their target water. In very shallow areas and when you're going over shallow tailout gravel bars, such rocks can also indicate the deepest water path, because the streambed around them tends to erode more deeply than the rest of the streambed. This is just one example of more tactical rowing strategies for low-water fishing.

Unnecessary pivoting and ferrying makes fishing decidedly more difficult and annoying, especially for the stern angler. Fly-line length has to be rapidly and frequently changed. Just as an angler is about to drop a fly on some hot spot, an overrowed boat can yank it away. It's the smoothest, straightest course you should row, one that allows anglers to use a steady length of fly line. You shouldn't be too near the target water, which scares fish, or so far as to make presentations difficult. There is usually an ideal distance to be maintained, and it does take a degree of constant awareness to maintain it. There's nothing more annoying than trying to fish from a poorly rowed boat.

The rowing technique I'm about to describe came naturally to me, but only after years of low-water rowing experience. Even today, more than 30 years later, it's rare for me to see anyone on the river other than guides using this rowing style.

The crawl stroke is a combination of two distinctly different rowing techniques: back rowing and sweeping. Sweeping is an old and localized method of rowing in which the oars are stationed at the front and rear of the boat, rather than at the sides. Such oars are so big and long that often one person rows each oar, and each rower may even need to stand. Sweeps were commonly used in the 1800s on various types of rafts (including bundled logs being navigated downstream to mills) and on flatboats such as those that took immigrants down the Ohio River in the days of early westward expansion. Some of these rafts and flatboats were quite large. The only rivers I'm aware of where sweep oars are seen today are in Idaho, where a few tour operators still use them on large rafts.

Naturally, a boat with oars on the front and back can only be rowed sideways. Such craft go with the flow when out in the currents but are swept sideways with the oars to the slower inside bends and eddies in order to land and to dodge hazards.

Big rafts and sweep boats used by the pioneers might have had oars on the sides as well as the ends, plus poles to push with off the bottom, and perhaps even a sail. Pioneer and fur-trading history makes for some very interesting reading, for these boaters not only drifted down into uncertain waters and futures but also had to contend with storms, floods, ice, Native Americans whose lands they were trespassing on, and even organized bands of river pirates.

The crawl stroke combines back rowing with sweeping. The end result is that you can row the boat sideways while keeping it parallel to the banks. This rowing technique eliminates a high percentage of standard pivot turns, making it easier for anglers, and especially the stern angler, to fish. It's the stern angler who's affected most by maneuvering, because the stern is the end being pivoted and redirected the most. The stern angler also has to cast over the oars, something we'll look at later. The boatman is usually rowing to position the bow angler in the best location, with the stern angler working with whatever boat angle is handed to him. This is why the crawl stroke is so good for fishing. Both anglers can be kept in the best possible position more of the time. The crawl is also a smooth oar stroke. Because the boat is nothing more than a platform for anglers to cast from, the steadier and smoother one can row it, the better its fishing potential.

Here's how the crawl stroke works. As you back-row with one hand (the left one in the illustration), you sweep with the right one. Sweeping pushes water sideways under the boat rather than parallel to its course. This is achieved by pointing the right oar forward rather than to the side (this calls for a change in hand position), dipping it in the water a couple of feet to the bow side of the boat, and then pushing on it. This feels unnatural at first. You'll probably have trouble grasping the concept initially. It's a lot like the old rub your belly while patting your head routine. It does take practice to make it come naturally.

The crawl stroke combines back rowing with one hand and pushing outward or sweeping with the other. The back of the boat must be cocked slightly in the direction you want to go, about 15 degrees. The end result is that you can row the boat sideways, something you might have not thought possible. It doesn't feel natural at first, and it takes a little practice.

There are a couple of prerequisites to doing the crawl. First, the boat needs to be cocked slightly, with the stern angled in the direction you're crawling (which is the direction you want to go) about 15 degrees. This calls for a very minor pivot before the first crawl stroke can be made, and one that doesn't interrupt the fishing.

The second element that's necessary is an oarlock that's positioned at the widest point of the boat's gunwale, but it's even better if it actually protrudes out beyond the boat's sides. This configuration is most commonly found on rafts where the metal rowing frame and oarlock stands stick out sideways beyond the raft's tubes. The farther beyond the side of the boat the oarlock is fabricated (within reason), the more effective the crawl, because the oarsman can then push water farther sideways under the bow of the boat.

An oarsman doing the crawl stroke looks a little ungainly at first sight. He leans sideways rhythmically with each oar stroke, twisting his body somewhat, rather than leaning back. This is due to the pushing out on the crawling or sweeping oar that pushes the water sideways under the boat. He pulls on one oar while pushing sideways with the other.

There's no doubt that this rowing style is harder on wrists and elbows, and after more than 30 years of rowing, mine are starting to give me some problems. This is not a rowing style that's powerful enough for heavy-water maneuvering or strong crosswinds, either. It is ideal for fishing and for subtle maneuvering around rocks, and it largely eliminates those strong pivot turns that give the stern angler casting problems. I'd say I use the crawl stroke at least 50 percent of the rowing day and perhaps 75 percent of the time on low-water, rock-dodging rivers. It's that effective.

The crawl stroke has a couple of other practical uses, too. The first one comes in handy for "grabbing eddies." When I pass a boulder or island and wish to pull in behind it, my downstream-pointed sweep oar is grabbed by the back-swirling eddy water, which helps pull the boat in.

Another case involves the eddies found on the inside bends of rivers, which are also good places to find a fish or two. I use this application most on small rivers, when I don't want to get swept out to the outside bend or undercut bank side, where the current naturally tends to go. After the anglers pop a couple of quick casts ahead of the boat and into the eddy line and eddy, the boatman can use this eddy line to help navigate a sharp bend in the river. There also tend to be fish along the outside of the bend, where deeper, swifter water is generally found, with some good big fish-holding pockets. As the rower approaches

THE CRAWL STROKE

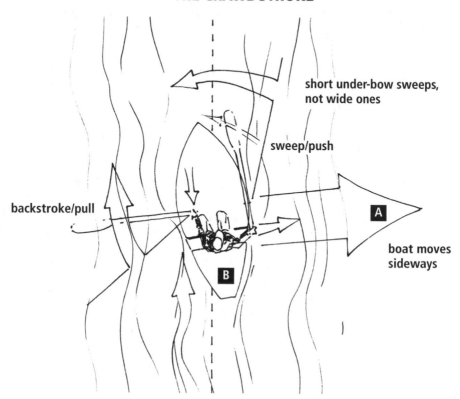

short under-bow sweeps, not wide ones

sweep/push

backstroke/pull

A

boat moves sideways

B

A. The crawl stroke allows a boat to be rowed sideways while still being slowed for fishing. One oar is pulled as usual; the other is pointed downstream and is pushed.

B. The stern is cocked to about a 15-degree angle to the current and points slightly in the direction the boat will travel.

the river's bend and perceives the need to start powering away from the fast water outside the bend, he can do a slight pivot as needed, and then begin crawling over toward the inside bend. Anglers will want to give their attention to the inside bend before the boat floats through it with some almost straight downstream casts. By crawling over to the inside-point eddy

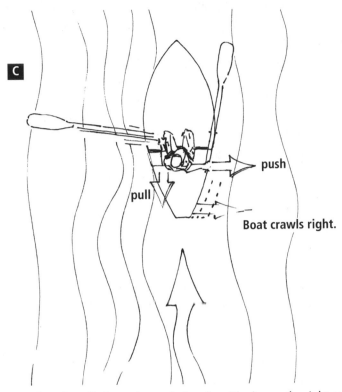

push

pull

Boat crawls right.

C. The crawl stroke calls for a change in hand positioning as the right oar in the illustration swings into a sweeping position. The oar is then dipped and pushed rather than pulled. The sweep stroke is a short one but enough to move the boat sideways toward the sweep-oar side.

line, the boat will be in a good position to slow down while switching the fishing focus to the outside bank. The sweeping oar, which is pointing downstream on the inside-bend side, will be grabbed somewhat by the eddying water there. This actually helps draw the boat into the eddy, turning it naturally, and often matches the curve of the bend in the river. The boat turns on its own with the sweep oar producing a ruddering effect as it's caught in the inside-bend eddy. This is clearer on the river, once you've played with it, than it sounds on paper. I use this dodge frequently.

When rowing on more powerful whitewater rivers, the crawl stroke isn't always strong enough. Quickly revert back to the pivot and back-row style in this situation.

One thing you do have to watch for and be aware of when crawling is the depth of the water and the presence of rocks. This is especially true when you're crawling over to shallower inside bends. Because the oar is pointed straight downstream, it can and does jam into the bottom on occasion, with the weight of the boat bearing down on it. Because most oarlocks allow the oar to come free in this situation, one must keep a grip on the oar so it doesn't fall overboard. Most oarlock systems do have a retentive feature to keep the oars from coming off too easily. What can happen, though, is that oar blades can fracture and break. I've also had oar blades jam straight in between rocks so tightly that I could hardly get them back out, especially once the boat starts spinning out of control in the currents, levering the oar blade in even tighter. I've snapped a few blades in this fashion over the years. I'm sure this presents a rather comic scene to bystanders: me standing and yanking on the oar and yelling at it while spinning in circles and stuck midstream. In any case, remain aware of river depth and bottom structure when crawling in the shallows and dip quickly.

One last application of the crawl stroke is hugging the banks in very narrow channels where going down the middle would eliminate most of the fishing possibilities. This usually occurs when a small river is broken up into several channels by islands. Rowing the usual way calls for enough water to the sides of the boat for full oar extension, as well as enough depth to gain a scoop of water. Get too close, and the oar hits the bottom or the bank itself.

USING THE CRAWL STROKE WITH EDDIES

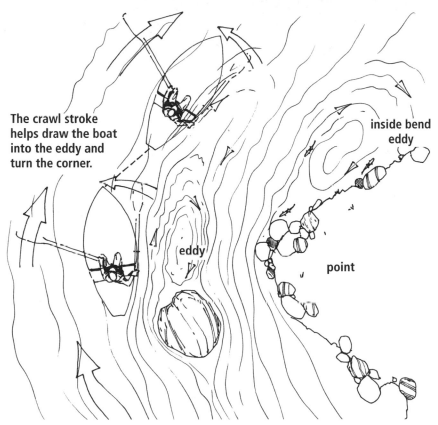

The crawl stroke helps draw the boat into the eddy and turn the corner.

inside bend eddy

eddy

point

Because a boat coming down the main current is going faster than the currents in an eddy (some of which are actually going back upstream), the sweeping oar has a pronounced front-ruddering effect. The boat tends to go in the direction in which the submerged sweep oar is pointing. (To the right, in the illustration. Continued backstrokes with the left oar will be needed to keep the boat from spinning in a circle.) You'll feel a heavy pull on the sweep oar as it grabs those currents and gets sucked into the eddy. In very powerful rivers this will be too hard on your arm, so quickly revert to normal pivoting and back rowing. Otherwise, the crawl stroke helps steer you into eddies and around corners with a minimum of pivot turns.

The crawl stroke allows you to hug banks more closely, and in this case, a gravel bar. This comes in handy when you want to fish the middle of the river, rather than the banks.

The crawl stroke allows you to move in closer to a bank with the sweeping oar parallel to the bank side. It works more as a rudder here, with only short little corrective strokes possible, but they are usually enough. Here again, the water eddies, this time off the edges of the bank. The sweep oar draws that boat in toward the bank. The outer oar can be pulled or just planted to maintain some forward progress while keeping the craft parallel to the shore.

Another use of the sweeping oar comes in here—that of pushing the water away from the boat, instead of underneath it, while crawling. This reverse crawl is usually necessary when slinking along close to a bank, because the river's current tends to push the boat, and especially the front of the boat, into the bank. We're generally dealing with mild edge-water currents in such cases, and this application of the crawl and reverse crawl works well in these situations. Just be sure to watch how deeply you dig your sweeping blade, because you're hovering in the shallows. Each dig of the crawling oar should be shallow and quick, perhaps burying only half the blade in the water.

This bank-hugging technique is used most when there are miles yet to be floated, for otherwise, time allowing, it would be better to pull over, anchor, and wade-fish small side channels. If

HUGGING A BANK WITH THE CRAWL STROKE

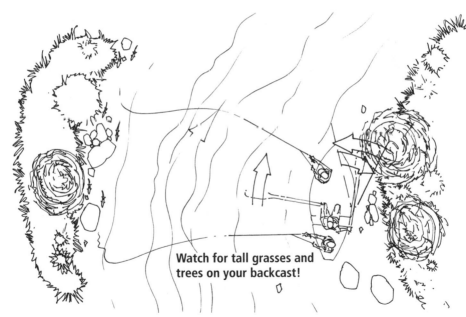

Watch for tall grasses and trees on your backcast!

The crawl stroke allows you to hug a bank more closely than you can rowing conventionally. I find this most useful when floating through small side channels that I don't have the time or desire to stop and wade-fish. In this way I can still fish the middle and far bank without floating down the middle and scaring all the fish in the channel. The sweep oar can push water either way for fine maneuvering. It often scrapes the bottom, as might the boat, being in such close proximity to the bank.

you need to keep some forward progress going, though, hugging the banks allows anglers to continue fishing the middle and far side of a small channel. Their casts might need to be more downstream and ahead of the boat than normal, though, so that the trout see the fly before they see the boat. Watch out for tall streamside foliage behind you. It's best to look back before each backcast when hugging the banks.

STANDARD CRAWL STROKE
Step 1
As always, observe and assess the rowing course and hazards as early as possible (see the illustration).

Step 2
Make a very easy pivot by dragging the right oar for a second while continuing to back-row once or twice with the left. You're only looking to achieve about a 15- to 20-degree angle against the current here, which isn't enough to really interfere with the stern angler's casting. As soon as the boat achieves this slight angle, lift the right oar from the water and swing it till the blade is pointing downstream. This calls for a switch of the arm and hand position on the oar, and a posture that's somewhat like leaning against the handrail of a staircase or escalator.

Step 3
This is the tricky part for beginners. Continue back-rowing with the left oar while you sweep with the right. The 15- to 20-degree cant of the boat to the current is maintained throughout. Make the sweep stroke by dipping the oar blade in the water a couple of feet out from the boat's bow side, and then push the oar handle outward with your arm until the blade almost hits the front side of the boat. Then quickly lift it from the water and sweep it back out for the next oar stroke. This pushes water mostly sideways under the craft, with the oar also acting

STANDARD CRAWL STROKE

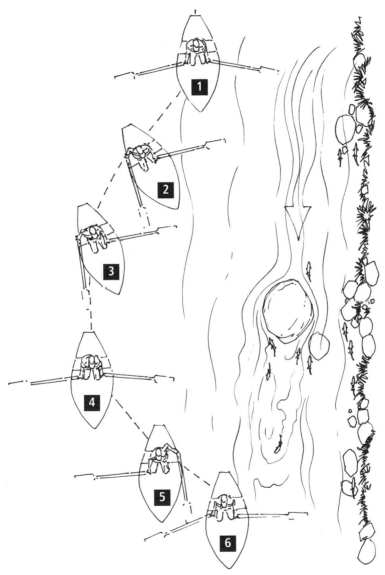

Slight 15-degree pivots and the crawl stroke ease this craft around a boulder, keeping it at the proper casting distance.

somewhat as a front-end rudder, or steering device. The stroke with the sweep-oar arm is usually enhanced with a little sideways body English, with the rower leaning into the oar for greater leverage, because this is a relatively weak arm position.

Step 4

Once you've crawled or side-rowed your boat out far enough to miss and fish the boulder, straighten up by dragging your left oar, switching your right-hand grip back to a normal rowing position, and making one or two right-hand backstrokes.

If it seems as though the crawl stroke isn't moving you sideways fast enough to miss the boulder, immediately pivot the stern farther out to the ferrying angle with your left oar, reset the right oar to a normal back-rowing position, and heave on both oars to get out of the area. Quick decisions and good early judgment are always advised. With practice, though, you'll find that you can crawl to the side of most river obstacles in mellower flows.

Step 5

After fishing in front, along the sides, and behind the boulder, angle the stern 15 to 20 degrees back toward the shore by dragging your left oar and pulling a couple of times on the right. Reposition the left-hand oar grip to the sweeping position, and crawl your way back to bank-fishing range.

Step 6

Drag the right oar, reposition the left hand to the normal back-rowing position, and pull a couple of times on the left oar to straighten and float-fish your way down the bank. The crawl is especially beneficial for maintaining the same distance from the bank, even when there are no obstacles to row around. I'll crawl back and forth by small increments all day.

At first glance, it might seem that all this hand and oar position changing might be more work than it's worth. For me, that's not the case. When I am rowing, there is plenty of added hand and oar maneuvering going on, sometimes every five to ten seconds. It looks a little more frantic to an observer (such as the angler in the stern of my boat). The end result, however, and the one I as a guide am considering most, is that it greatly modifies the effects of pivot turns, keeping a smoother, steadier course. This allows better opportunities for both bow and stern anglers.

Another plus from the stern angler's point of view is that when a rower is crawling, he doesn't have to contend with the oar as much. In normal back-rowing situations, the stern angler has to cast over the oar a good percentage of the time, holding his rod up a bit to allow the oar to pass underneath it. Tangles of oars and the stern angler's fly line are common otherwise. With the crawl stroke, the sweeping oar is pointed forward, often on the side being fished, and it is out of the way of both anglers' fly lines. The stern angler does, however, have to be aware of changes in oar positioning as the rower switches styles to meet current demands.

I use the crawl stroke a lot for subtle distance compensations, even when no real obstacles are in the way. There are many other factors that affect a boat's position in relation to the banks, including crosswinds, crosscurrents, and bends in the river (which usually concentrate currents to the deeper, outside shore of the bend). To keep the perfect distance away from a bank (or other target water), say, 40 to 50 feet, requires constant attention to and adjustment for these factors. Most can be anticipated, preassessed, and set up for. When you are rowing anglers, more time is usually spent repositioning the boat to maintain an ideal casting position than in avoiding obstacles. This is where the crawl stroke is so valuable.

THE PIVOT TURN AND STERN ANGLER

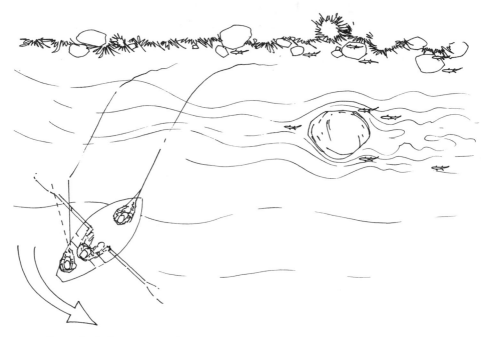

The typical pivot turn used to row around an obstacle affects the stern angler in two ways. First, it swings his end of the boat farther away from the target water, dragging his fly from it. Second, his line and the oar (the left one in the illustration) now cross paths. Tangles between the two are common. The stern angler must lift his rod and line to allow the oar to pass underneath it. This is another reason why the crawl stroke can be advantageous for rowing anglers.

For instance, if the wind has blown you sideways a bit (a common occurrence in the West), you can make an almost imperceptible pivot and then crawl your way back to the proper distance from shore and straighten. Passengers hardly notice you're doing it. Compare this to the back-rowing method, where the boat is pivoted at a greater angle, back-rowed a few

UNDERWATER BACKSTROKE

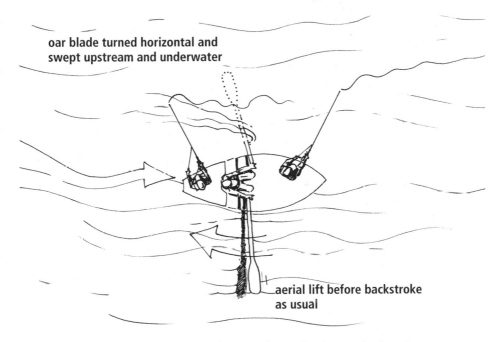

oar blade turned horizontal and
swept upstream and underwater

aerial lift before backstroke
as usual

If the stern angler's fly line is in the rower's way for the next backstroke, turn
the blade horizontally (with horn oarlocks) and sweep it back upstream
under the fly line. Do not lift the blade from the water.

strokes, and pivoted again. This affects the stern fisherman
more, and it jostles both anglers to a greater degree.

Most of the time, I cock the boat slightly and position one
oar or the other to sweep almost continuously. Crawl right a
bit, then back left, perhaps back-rowing with both oars for a
little while, then back to a right crawl, and so it goes all day.
I'm rowing for a paying angler's pleasure and perhaps putting
out a more concentrated effort for a greater part of the day than
the average recreational floater would. But once you are used to
the crawl stroke, it will prove to be an ideal rowing technique

for the fine-tuned positioning of a fishing boat, despite its ungainly appearance.

There is one more aspect of the crawl stroke that I find important in mid to late summer, when rivers are very low. Currents have slowed, rock evasion is frequently necessary, and the time it takes to get down a long reach of river has increased dramatically when compared with the high-water flows of spring and early summer. In these conditions, the crawl stroke allows side-to-side maneuvering without slowing to the degree the normal backrowing technique does. This may sound like a small point, but being able to gauge your speed and mileage over a particular stretch of time is an art. If you want to float a 15-mile stretch from 7 A.M. to 6 P.M., fish it hard, and not have to row out late in the dark or row through several miles of perfect water because you wasted too much time early on, you need to know how to gauge your progression over the course of the day. Getting to the take-out earlier than planned can be just as bad as getting in way too late, in the eyes of an angler. Arriving on time and maximizing the fishing potential within the allotted time takes plenty of experience.

In low-water rock-dodging extremes, the crawl stroke allows me to maneuver efficiently yet keep the boat moving forward enough to keep to my schedule. I go slow enough to fish well but don't bog down to a near standstill by using backstroke maneuvering. On some of my backcountry multiday float trips, I have some long-mileage, low-water days. The experienced guides will make it down to camp at just the right time for dinner. New and inexperienced boatmen will get to camp too early, too late, or even after dark. Of course, if a great hatch and super fishing slowed them down, it's okay!

How hard you back-row varies with water level. The high-water season calls for a vigorous back-rowing pace so you don't blow through a day's fishing water in half a day. High water can also mean greatly reduced wade-fishing potential, with more time and mileage spent fishing from the boat. Back rowing like mad early in the season is tough on your muscles and hands.

Low water presents the opposite problem—too much good-looking and wadable water with too many slow-flowing miles of river left to go. It's here that the easy-paced crawl stroke comes in so handy. It allows a steadier forward progress, when desired. If your chosen daily mileage can't be adjusted, your rowing pace and style must make up for it.

3

Avoiding River Hazards

Many of the world's most productive trout rivers are easily navigated. Although hazards exist, they are capably handled by knowledgeable and observant rowers. Most of the actual oar time is spent slowing and positioning the boat to improve fishing. Nevertheless, an understanding of river hazards and the power of moving water is a must for all floaters.

The majority of river drownings are due to ignorance of river conditions, poor rowing or paddling skills, or insufficient or inadequate equipment. Rivers don't always give you the luxury of time to debate varied and sundry rowing options as they shove you toward a logjam. You need to understand the inherent qualities of moving water and its response to obstacles in its path. Water will shape streambeds in a predictable sequence of bends, riffles, and pools until it meets solid bedrock, tumbled boulders, and timber fall. Knowing how moving water responds to such impediments makes decision making quicker and navigation surer.

An experienced rower, for instance, will know that a sharp bend in a river will concentrate a stronger flow to the outside

Rowers need to sum up river hazards and fishing possibilities. Avoiding mishaps while keeping anglers in a good position is the name of the game.

bend of the corner. He'll instinctively spin his stern toward the inside bend and start back-rowing toward it before getting into the bend itself. A novice often lets the river almost shove him into the outside-bend bank before rowing like mad at the last second to pull away. It's a preassessment of what the water is likely to do that allows experienced boatmen to set up, which is the all-important element of more technical rowing.

The hazards we'll discuss are common on many rivers. Additional water volume (high water to flood stage) and current speed will increase navigational difficulties. Extreme low water makes it hard to get a blade full of water at times, which also makes maneuvering difficult with oars. Bouncing off a low-water rock just before entering a tricky chute can throw you totally off course. In any case, treat all hazards with respect. Observe them coming, plan your route, and with the techniques described in Chapters 1 and 2, set up your boat in advance. With the proper assessment and setup, the avoidance maneuver itself often requires just a few well-timed oar strokes to skirt you around a hazard.

THE BASIC MANEUVER AROUND A RIVER HAZARD

The diagram and steps that follow describe a basic sequence of maneuvers for negotiating a path around a river hazard. Further complexities can arise when crosscurrents, side winds, heavy water and turbulence, or multiple rock maneuvers become involved. Though these factors add challenges that call for more thought, the basic rowing maneuvers remain the same.

Step 1

The first step in navigating an obstacle is to *clearly recognize its presence* early on and *plan your upcoming route* and the maneuvering needed to follow it. This should be formulating as soon as the hazard comes into view, not when the boat is pressed up face-to-face with it.

Step 2

When you have recognized the danger and figured out the preferred route around it (to the midriver side in the illustration), the boat is pivot-turned or set up by pulling back on the left oar several times while planting the right oar or pushing forward on it once or twice. The boat is now angled properly to begin a back-rowing ferry out of the rock's path and toward midriver, about 45 degrees.

Step 3

Several backstrokes with both oars now build up enough momentum to ferry the boat out of the rock's path. In many cases, this will require only three to six oar strokes. In a twist-

THE BASIC MANEUVER AROUND A RIVER HAZARD

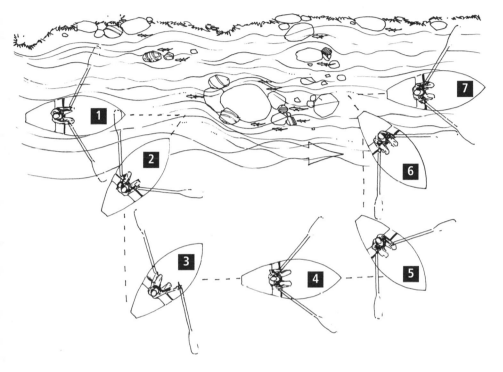

ing river with powerful currents, it might take several more. At the same time, you're still trying to slow down the boat and put anglers in a good position to fish around the boulder, the bank, or both. There are times, of course, when safety will override fishing considerations, and the boat may have to be rowed away from the best theoretic fishing position. On the other hand, beginning rowers do have a tendency to row farther away from an obstacle than necessary, making fishing more difficult. Only experience will teach you how many oar strokes you will need to move the boat a certain distance in a particular current. It can take as few as two to four backstrokes to move the boat far enough after pivoting. In any case, remember that the stern of the boat should always point away from the obstacle and toward the best escape route as you approach it. Pointing the stern straight up-current is not the correct ferrying angle!

Step 4

After ferrying to the midriver side of the rock (smoothly, so as not to jostle passengers more than necessary) and lining up in a good fishing drift lane to go by it, straighten the boat in the current by pulling a few times on the right oar while you plant and drag the left. This will straighten you back up. Now continue an easy back-rowing pace to slow the craft down as you float-fish your way on by it. Fish are likely to be found upstream, tucked right along the sides, and in the eddy line and downstream eddy of midriver boulders. Don't neglect to run a fly by all these locations in succession. In a slow- to medium-flowing river, the oarsman can back-row the boat to a standstill, allowing a few extra drifts of the flies, or even anchor there, if you see rising fish in the eddy. Anglers should be consciously targeting different spots for maximum teamwork efficiency. This can be agreed to prior to the approach, thus keeping the two anglers from jamming out their casts to the same spot at the same time, which some trout find unnerving!

Step 5

Having gone by the rock and now intending to get back to the fish-sheltering banks, pivot the boat again so that the stern points at a 45-degree angle toward shore. This is done by pulling on the right oar several times while planting or pushing forward on the left oar.

Step 6

Once you have angled the boat properly, a few pulls on both oars should get you back in casting range of the bank. Eddies behind rocks help suck the boat in behind them, too, which can reduce the number of oar strokes you need to realign with the bank. On whitewater stretches, you can use these eddies in various ways to enhance navigation, to slow the boat down, or even come to a standstill, allowing a little rest while you scrutinize the rowing path yet to come. Eddies can act as midriver parking spots, or at least places to slow down, giving you a moment to plot your next strategic ferrying move.

When water is pouring over boulders, these more turbulent eddies become known as holes. We'll discuss these on page 66, for they can be dangerous and easily flip boats. Don't cut in too closely behind large-volume flows over big boulders. They tend to suck a boat quickly in right behind them, spin it sideways, fill it with water, and perhaps flip it.

Step 7

Once you have ferried the boat back to the desired distance from shore, drag the right oar and pull back a few times on the left. This straightens the boat out again so that you are in good shape to continue fishing along the banks. Keep a steady but not too taxing back-rowing pace to improve the fishing possibilities. During this whole sequence, the stern angler is most affected by the pivoting. He must avoid the back-swept oar, lifting his rod and line to let the oar pass under it.

On rock-studded rivers, maneuvering will be constant, varied, and fun. Once it becomes second nature, you'll find you can row, look for rising fish, and duck bad casts simultaneously, all while analyzing the best rowing route and most likely fish-holding water.

WRAPPING BOULDERS AND FLIPPING IN HOLES

Having discussed the basic rowing maneuver to ferry around a rock or boulder, we'll now look at what happens if you actually hit one. We'll also take a close look at the hole water creates when it pours over barely submerged boulders and ledges.

What commonly happens when a raft or drift boat hits a boulder is (1) a sudden impact occurs that can be more jolting than you might imagine and that can knock people out of their seats and toss gear overboard; (2) the boat might just bounce and spin off the rock, creating the possibility of dislodging, losing overboard, or even breaking an oar; and (3) the boat can flip or wrap around the boulder.

When a boat slams into a boulder, it's usually because the boatman didn't set up and begin a back-rowing ferry away from it early enough in the game. (In some rock-choked channels it's impossible not to hit a rock or two.) The boat will hit most boulders at some sort of a sideways angle, with the rower making a last-ditch attempt to pull away from it. Occasionally, the boat plows nose-first into a boulder. This tends to happen with novices who are completely out of control, or it happens in tight rock gardens when obstacles are coming at you so fast that any mistake is likely to get you in trouble. It's not unusual to be rowing down a rocky channel and blow out an oar by jamming it into a shallow rock. The time it takes to reposition an oar in the oarlock in such a case can be just long enough to totally foul up your route and setup, resulting in a pinball escapade where the boat bounces through the rest of the run. I occasionally hit rocks while watching my anglers' dry flies dancing along on the currents (I like to watch trout take them as much as the anglers do). The front ends of drift boats are high enough to block much of the forward view, especially when the bow angler is standing up and casting. You may have to pivot occasionally just to look around him. In rock-dodging runs, you must pay extra attention to every detail of the channel.

Slamming into rocks can easily send loose pieces of equipment on the deck of a drift boat or the sides of a raft overboard. Many rods, cameras, and the like are lost and sunk every year. If you know you're about to enter a challenging bit of water, tie down and secure all gear and put on life jackets. Though most

COLLISIONS WITH BOULDERS

When a boat slams into a river-washed boulder, a predictable sequence of events can rapidly follow. The greater the speed and force of the water, the more likely the boat is to flip or wrap. The impact can be more jarring than you'd expect. Gear and people can fly overboard. Water instantly begins heaving up and possibly over the upstream side. This tends to shove it under the surface, possibly pinning the craft to the rock beneath tons of moving water. Although a boat can flip the other way, most flip and wrap with the hull side to the rock. Luckier craft just bounce and spin off, some half full of water.

fly fishermen don't like to wear life jackets because they interfere with casting and comfort, one should at least have the common sense to know when to put them on.

The biggest danger in slamming into boulders is that rafts or drift boats can be flipped or wrapped. Rafts are more forgiving than drift boats in this regard, and many novice floaters prefer them as the best all-purpose craft. A river will apply tons of water pressure to a boat that's wrapped around the upstream side of a boulder. Often it's impossible to get the boat back off

Pulling a wrapped raft off a boulder takes long ropes and lots of manpower. The aid of other floaters might have to be enlisted to apply enough force.

without a lot of extra manual or mechanical help. Many boats are abandoned as total losses in such situations, along with much of the equipment aboard. It's possible for people to get pinned between the boat and rock, too, drowning them.

Extra people, long ropes, winches, or even a motor vehicle might be needed to dislodge a wrapped boat from the current's grip. There are a few other tricks of the trade that we'll look at shortly, too. In some cases, you might not be able to free the boat until the river drops a little. Hard-hull drift boats often buckle, collapsing around boulders. Rafts are more likely to be rescued intact because of their flexibility, but they can suffer damages to their tubes, floors, and rowing frames.

Wraps usually produce panicked anglers floating and struggling downstream, scurrying to round up and save as much equipment as possible, and frequently suffering cuts and bruises as well as hypothermia in cold water and weather. On long-mileage river expeditions, such situations spell total disaster. You might have to hike out a canyon for miles to reach the nearest ranch or depend on the generosity of other floaters to pick you up and take your party out. This could ruin their long-planned yearly river vacation, too. Experienced river runners are not always thrilled to bail out novices if being under-equipped or underskilled was a major factor in the emergency. Serious first aid can be an hour or two away at minimum, and sometimes an entire day.

When a boat plows into a boulder, the following sequence of events usually unfolds.

A sudden jolt sends equipment flying and can knock people out of their seats. The impact can be harder than imagined. Very often people in the boat will lean away from the rock in fear, which, as we'll see shortly, can be opposite what they need to do. Human nature often leads the inexperienced and unlearned to do the wrong things in moving-water situations.

The water that was plowing into the upstream side of the boulder is now surging against the upstream side of your boat. It tends to climb rapidly up and over it and start to shove it underwater. The heavier and faster the water, the quicker this will take place. If the passengers on board lean away from the rock in fear (a natural reaction), they just help to sink the upstream side of the boat all the quicker. At this point, the boat could wrap around the rock, getting pinned there, or it might fill partially with water, bounce and spin off the rock, and continue down the river, either right side up or upside down. It's also possible in turbulent water for a boat to wrap so that passengers become pinned between the boat and the rock. This happens much less often and usually in rougher rivers with surging currents. It can take superhuman rescue efforts to retrieve those in such immediate peril, calling for split-second decision making and action.

When you find yourself about to be side-slammed into a boulder, take whatever last-ditch evasive actions are possible

AVOIDING A FLIP ON A BOULDER

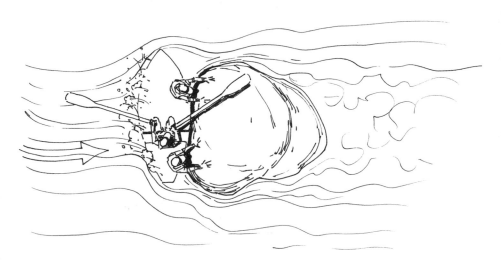

The upstream end tends to get shoved underwater.

Once seriously engaged, the rower continues to stroke like mad, trying to spin the boat off the rock. Leaning away from the rock in fear just before impact tends to increase the chances of a flip. Passengers should move toward the high side in an effort to keep the boat from flipping. The boat could be filling with water at this point, and rowing could be of little help. Don life jackets now if you haven't already done so.

and then be ready to use human weight as ballast, counteracting the boat's tendency to roll, flip, and wrap. This takes quick and determined action, which is helped immensely by forethought.

Just before hitting the rock, try to get in a last strong oar stroke or two to get the boat going to one side or the other of the boulder as much as possible. In this way, you're more likely to bounce and spin off the obstruction, rather than broadsiding it. What most experienced boatmen do is continue using the upstream oar to make powerful levering sweeps, trying to spin the boat off the boulder before it starts to wrap. Some will even try to get a spin going on the boat before it hits the rock, hoping for a pinball deflection (which can be quite jolting).

Because boats usually end up pinned sideways to rocks, the downstream oar is likely to be wedged uselessly against the boulder or blown out of the oarlock and rendered inoperable. The upstream oar needs to be used with a vengeance to pry and spin the boat off the rock before it starts to fill with water and wrap.

At the same time, experienced floaters will know that the upstream side of the boat is likely to get shoved underwater, which causes the wrap or flip. What they'll instinctively do is lean into the rock, using their body weight as ballast in fighting the boat's tendency to be pushed under. Human ballast is an important aspect of whitewater rowing. Even anglers might need to resort to it to save the boat and equipment in a pinch (because anglers don't expect flips and don't tie their equipment in).

Because water is pushing the upstream side of the boat down and underwater, the downstream side tends to be lifted a bit. It's here that human weight needs to be applied to counteract a flip. All the while, the oarsman should continue to row like mad, trying to lever and spin the boat off one side or the other. Most often, it will come free. In easy flows, there might be no consequences. In heavier currents, it's likely that the boat

REMOVING A BADLY WRAPPED RAFT

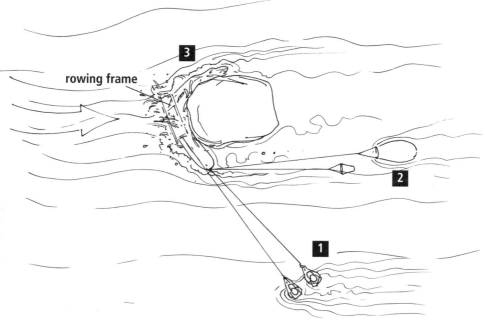

rowing frame

Wrapped rafts can be very difficult to pull off rocks.

1. Enough people pulling on long ropes can do the job, presuming you have ropes along.

2. Buckets and other gear can be hung off ropes and straps for added pull in the current.

3. Deflating one side of the raft, or even cutting the floor open on one side, might be necessary to loosen the river's grip on the boat. This depends on your ability to get back out to the raft, of course.

will have shipped a lot of water that will need to be bailed (unless you have a self-bailing raft). It can also roll over and flip before coming loose, which necessitates a major rehab operation. There may be equipment or people that got washed overboard to be rounded up. Broken oars are another possibility. You always need to bring extra oars, oarlocks, patch kits, and first-aid kits on challenging rivers, along with a pump for rafts. In addition, life jackets, ropes, and a list of other equipment should be taken on every trip down a river. We'll look at this more closely in Chapter 6.

If the boat does wrap and stick, you have some quick decisions to make. You might want to round up as much equipment as possible before it floats downstream beyond recovery. Any serious injuries need to be dealt with and a rescue plan implemented. Hypothermia can be a real threat. Anyone routinely involved in outdoor sports should take first-aid and CPR classes at regular intervals.

The ability to pull a wrapped boat off a boulder can depend on having a long rope. This may need to be rescued from the wrapped boat before it can be used. The rope must be attached securely to the boat at the end that is most likely to free the wrap. This usually means that someone will have to go upstream a bit, swim down to the raft, grab on, and tie the rope in place. This isn't always easy, safe, or possible. Freezing cold water is especially daunting and dangerous.

Even getting the rope attached doesn't mean that three people can pull the boat off a boulder. A strong current can apply several tons of pressure on the boat. If the boat is but lightly balanced on the rock, it might come off with a few hard pulls. If another boating party drifts by, enlist their aid, too. It could take a dozen or more people to do the job. Of course, if you don't carry a 50-foot heavy-duty rope for such occasions, you'll just be standing there dripping wet with a blank stare on your face. Few anglers go forth with whitewater boaters' precautions, because flipping isn't in their game plan. Being rescue-equipped, however, isn't a bad idea, even if you know your river. The river always seems to come up with new ways to test your skills, equipment, and vehicles!

There are a few other ploys to use with rafts. These also rely on your being able to get back to your boat and wrestle (literally) with the problem. Deflating half of the raft can loosen the river's grip, making it easier to pull the inflated side off. Some boaters have tied ropes to the inflated end and connected buckets, waterproof bags, or whatever else might be on hand. These items drag downstream in the current, adding more pull. This can be critical when human helpers are in short supply. In some cases, boaters slit the raft floor at one end, allowing water to pour through the raft, which lessens the wrapping effect. These added efforts, plus enough force on the rope, can free a badly wrapped boat. Though repairs are likely to be needed, at least you have a boat to continue on with.

A wrapped drift boat gives you fewer options, for even more water weight is likely to be holding it in place. On the other hand, a drift boat's hull is more curved, allowing it to be rocked and pulled off boulders easily at times. Its floor, too, is slipperier than a raft's. In some cases, the hull will collapse around a rock, leaving the boat a near-total loss.

If you leave a boat wrapped around a rock and walk out, it's your responsibility to go back with help and get it off later, perhaps when the water level has dropped a bit. It's just river garbage now; you are guilty of littering, and you can be fined! Besides, there's almost always equipment of value to be salvaged. There are even experts at river-boat salvage because of the frequency with which expensive boats are wrapped and sunk on some of the more powerful western steelhead and trout rivers that flow to the Pacific.

Holes

When water pours over the top of barely submerged boulders, it creates what's known as a hole in whitewater circles. This is, of course, completely different from a fishing hole. The presence and intensity of holes vary in differing water levels. At low water, a boulder might be poking high above the surface and need to be rowed around. At medium to high water, the river

Holes or reversals in rivers can be isolated behind one boulder, or they can be half the river wide beneath a ledge. Big ones can easily spin boats sideways and then flip them over, giving floaters a nasty swim. Look ahead for big humps of water with a flat spot just downstream. The elevation drop can hide the actual hole from view.

could be covering the boulder, creating a strong suck hole behind it. At flood stage, there could be a vicious boat-flipping hole in the same place. With enough water, both boulder and hole will be submerged. You might see only a series of standing waves in their place.

When a river pours over a boulder or ledge, the weight and inertia of the quick-flowing water force the main current down toward the bottom of the river. The water right behind the rock near the surface rushes back upstream to fill the void. This results in a turbulent backflow capable of flipping boats in the blink of an eye. The bigger and wider the hole and the greater the volume of water and distance it drops, the greater its effect on boats. A small boulder's hole can be easily punched through by a rowed craft. You can even park there, letting the sucking effect hold the boat in place. A big drop over a larger boulder or river-wide ledge can pose serious flip potential, especially to novices. Holes that don't look or sound bad can give the Maytag treatment to the unexpecting.

Usually when a boat drops over a rock or ledge into a big hole the boat speeds up a bit as it plunges over the drop in a quickening current. When the boat hits the big hole, it's slammed to an immediate halt by the turbulence that's rushing back upstream. This jolt alone can throw people and equipment from the boat in severe cases, so passengers should be holding on. If the forward (downstream) inertia of the boat doesn't push it through the turbulence and downstream, the backflow can spin it sideways and shove it upstream into the hole, just behind the rock. Here the water rushing down and over the boulder will fill and shove the upstream side of the boat under water. The turbulence pushing up from the downstream side helps push that side up and over. This double whammy by a powerhouse hole can flip a boat so fast that you won't know what hit you.

Even if the boat doesn't flip, it's likely to be held in the hole for a while and fill with water. The upstream-pushing turbulence constantly wants to shove the boat back into the heart of the hole. As it gains hundreds of pounds in shipped water, the boat is more likely to be washed out of the hole, though it then becomes much harder to effectively row.

Once you are in a hole and quickly realize that the water pouring over the boulder is likely to roll and flip your boat, passengers need to shift their weight to the downstream end or side of the craft to counteract that force. This can require the immediate action of everyone in the boat and probably a stern commander yelling the proper moves to stem disaster and panic.

HOLES BEHIND BOULDERS

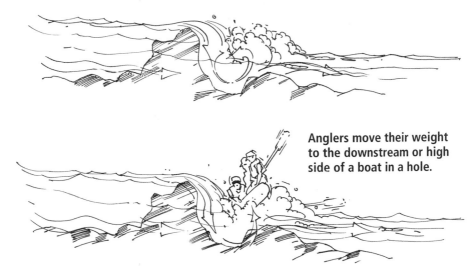

Anglers move their weight to the downstream or high side of a boat in a hole.

River water dropping over a boulder creates a hole downstream of it. The weight and velocity of the water dropping over the rock pushes its downstream current below the river's surface. A strong upstream surge of water fills this void. Boats caught here are spun sideways and are likely to be flipped by the down-and-up force of the hole. Rowing to escape and using human ballast are important to avoid flips. Boats often spin around and around in big holes, so passengers must be alert to the boat's position in the hole, moving themselves to counteract the boat's tendency to flip. The part of the boat closest to the hole-producing rock is the side that will be shoved under.

The rower's oars will probably be temporarily out of commission, because boats tend to be swung sideways and pushed up tight behind the boulder when in a hole. The turbulence and proximity of the rock can make rowing at this point very difficult, yet the boatman should continue trying to row his way out of the hole. The rest of the crew needs to use their weight as ballast to avoid a flip and should remain alert to the boat's position in the hole. Since boats slowly rotate in holes, you'll need to stay aware of the downstream end of the boat and reposition passengers there. The rower will be doing whatever he can with the oars but may also have to throw his weight around in critical moments. Drift boats will be less forgiving in holes: They lack the inherent flotation of rafts. Human ballast will be of even greater concern, and many drift boats will simply sink. Many have no flotation other than trapped air in storage compartments.

The water pouring over the boulder usually pours into the boat as well. This can wash unsecured equipment (and people) downstream. Once the boat fills with water, it's less likely to flip, though giant holes can flip anything. The boat's partially sunken weight tends to catch the deeper-flowing current that moves downstream. Eventually, it flounders out of the hole.

Holes can hold boats for a few seconds or for a minute or more. This depends on the size and shape of the hole, the drop, and the force of the water. A hole behind a narrow rock isn't likely to hold your boat very long, though it could possibly flip it and send you on your merry way downstream. A big wide boulder (say, 10 to 20 feet wide) or a wide ledge drop could hold you for quite a while. Boats can be flipped and rolled numerous times in killer holes and bashed around for several minutes. Often, floaters will be knocked out of the boat, wash free, and drift downstream while their raft continues to circulate. This is due to the raft's greater buoyancy and tendency to be held in the hole. A drift boat generally fills with water and sinks, getting washed out of the hole in less time. A sunk boat going down the river is likely to get beat up or pinned deep against a rock where it become very hard to retrieve.

Not having a life jacket on can be disastrous. In frothing whitewater and especially in holes, a person's head will be underwater as much or more than above, even when the person is wearing a life jacket. The vertically circulating water in a hole

spins you round and round. You often come back up to the surface under the boat, too, and have to scramble to get from
beneath it for a gasp of air. If all this sounds disconcerting, then
I'm making my point. You have to be alert enough to keep your
eyes open and see when your head is above water to take a
breath. Circulating in a nasty hole is very disorienting, too. A
quick spin and ejection from a hole will scare you a bit. A pro-
longed experience will scare you a lot. As soon as you are
ejected, shaking from adrenaline and cold water, you have to be
conscious enough to help others in your party or at least start
gathering up floating gear, as well as drag out the boat itself.

Although whitewater enthusiasts prepare for flips by wearing life jackets (and even wet suits and helmets) and carrying
safety and throw ropes, anglers generally do not. Experienced
whitewater floaters might even enjoy a flip. Float fishermen just
tend to panic, lose equipment, and occasionally drown.

The thing to do with holes is avoid them. On most fishing
waters, holes are easily missed with enough foresight and the
proper rowing skills. If you spy a big hump of water that looks
like a rounded heave and you can't see over it or what's downstream behind it, it's probably a hole. You'll often be going
down a concentrated chute filled with growing waves. Suddenly, you'll see a wave that's bigger than the rest, with dead
quiet water just downstream of it—the hole. Being upriver
blocks your view of many holes. They're hidden behind the
surge of water as it goes over the rock. The distance water falls
over a clean ledge can hide the view of the turbulent hole itself
in that case. You'll often hear the roar before seeing the rollback
wave. In some cases, ledge drops are hard to see coming
because the quiet flow upstream of the drop and the quiet
water just downstream of the turbulent hole blend together,
giving an illusion of a continuous stretch of flat water. If you
hear a roar but see nothing, it's time to quickly make for the
bank, get out of the boat, and scout out the situation. Any time

you see a piece of flat water ahead in the midst of concentrated currents and waves, it's likely that a rock and its hole are causing it.

Be alert and row around holes. When you're ferrying across a river, don't row in just behind big holes. They can actually suck you back upstream and flip you, just as surely as if you came down over them. Ferry behind such boulders where the water flattens out and has no appreciable upstream sucking flow. This is especially true with clean, wide ledge drops and man-made diversion dams, which can have amazing upstream tow, even when they don't look particularly dangerous.

If you are going to hit a big hole, make sure everybody puts on life jackets, secures what gear they can, and holds on tight. Hitting a hole head-on can be jolting. What the rower needs to do, once hitting a hole is deemed unavoidable, is build up as much downstream speed as possible. You want to blow through that heavy upstream-surging turbulence and push the boat downstream beyond its reversed flow. (Holes are also known as reversals.) If you see it coming early enough and can't avoid it, you might want to turn the boat around quickly and back-row downstream. This gives you more power and downstream speed both before you hit the hole and when you're in it. Don't try to spin the boat into the reverse position just as you're dropping into the hole, though, because being sideways to the hole is what you want to avoid most. If you find yourself suddenly face-to-face with a big hole, just row forward as hard and fast as you can to build maximum downstream inertia. Try your best to blast through.

Once in the hole, a boatman should row like mad to keep that downstream momentum going and to keep from getting spun sideways and sucked back into the drop. With enough downstream inertia and speed, you can power through small and medium-size holes. Monster holes are likely to eat you no

HIDDEN HOLES AND LEDGE DROPS

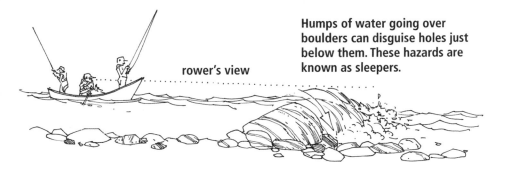

rower's view

Humps of water going over boulders can disguise holes just below them. These hazards are known as sleepers.

Many holes are hidden from the rower's view. You must learn to anticipate holes and ledge drops by what *can* be seen. A big drop in the river, flat water downstream of big waves or humps, and loud murmuring roars can announce upcoming holes. Part of your prefloat research should include pinpointing dangers on a detailed river map.

matter what. They can flip even big boats end-over-end or, as often happens, spin boats sideways, suck them in, and roll them over and over.

When a raft drops into a big hole, it can buckle and almost fold in half. Whitewater floaters make sure their boats are pumped tight to avoid this buckling effect. There have been cases of people's arms or legs getting trapped between the rowing frame and raft as the boat folds, only to be wedged there when it straightens back out—possibly upside down after a flip in the hole. Limbs have been broken and floaters knocked unconscious in these situations. People drown every year in big holes, ledges, and diversion dams. These are extreme cases but nevertheless are realities of floating strong rivers and missing the proper channels and chutes. Drift boats are less forgiving than rafts in most whitewater situations because they don't have the same flotation qualities and can flip rather quickly. On the other hand, they usually row better and respond faster to oar strokes. Whatever you row, treat big holes with plenty of respect.

LEDGES AND DIVERSION DAMS

Holes are taken a step further when water pours over a clean drop ledge or man-made diversion dam. Here the suction and flip effect of a hole can occur on a river-wide, inescapable scale. Even what appear to be short-drop diversion dams create some strong, all-consuming holes that don't look turbulent. Such holes are stronger than they appear. Though some can be rowed through with enough forward speed, many claim lives on a yearly basis. It's their innocent look, matched with an unrelenting backwash, that gets floaters and swimmers in trouble.

If you see sticks and flotsam sucked in and circulating just behind the drop of a straight-edged ledge or dam, take that as a serious hint that this hole doesn't like to let go of its possessions. Some diversion dams will hold debris for weeks.

DIVERSION DAM HOLES

Some diversion dams have rather innocent-looking but powerful bank-to-bank holes. Rotating debris in the vortex indicates a hole that doesn't like to let its objects go. This could include humans in life jackets. Avoid diversion-dam holes—portage around them. Some natural rock ledges have equally threatening and near-river-wide holes. Some killer holes may be identified on floaters' maps, but not all.

Although you can aim for navigable chutes that sometimes pour through broken ledges, river-wide ledges and dams should be scouted and portaged if you have any doubts about them. It's not worth flipping a boat and losing gear and possibly lives to pamper the ego of a novice or ignorant rower.

LOGJAMS

Sweepers (fallen trees) and logjams can present greater dangers than boulders in many cases. Water bounces off and deflects around boulders in what's known as a pillow. Logjams, on the other hand (also called "strainers") allow water to run through them. A boat or body can be pinned among the trunks and sharp limbs with a force beyond retrieval. The limbs can puncture raft tubes, even on glancing blows. Getting shoved into a logjam should be avoided at all costs. Portage a totally choked stretch of river if need be, and scout any channel in question.

LOGJAM DANGER

Whereas water must bounce off and go around individual boulders, it can sift through logjams without losing much speed. A boat or swimming angler pinned in a logjam can be in a serious, even life-threatening situation.

Sunk trees and logjams can be serious river hazards. The most dangerous time is just after a high-water period, when new jams can materialize in unexpected locations. By midsummer, many will have had a path around them chainsawed or eroded, but it can be a tight fit.

Individual logs and logjams can move from year to year. Early-season high and dropping river flows call for great caution. Once rivers settle into summer lows, channels usually become established around most logjams through erosion. Other floaters and fish and game departments often chainsaw bad ones out of the way on more popular rivers. If you are on a long expedition on a known logjammed river, it wouldn't hurt to carry a small chainsaw. It's easier than doing a major portage with lots of heavy gear.

Nonetheless, channels through many logjams can be narrow, requiring precise rowing. Protruding logs will interfere with some critical oar strokes. I find the crawl stroke to be most useful in some of these situations, because it allows me to pass obstacles more closely on the sweep-oar side. A novice shouldn't depend on the crawl stroke, however, before perfectly understanding it and its limitations.

Stop and scout bends in rivers where the full force of the current seems to plow into what appears as a river-wide log-jam. Though there will usually be a path through it, knowing the route beforehand can eliminate apprehension and possible misjudgment. These are often tight fits. As with all maneuvering, preplanning your route and setup is very important. The ability to make quick decisions, instant turns, and last-second maneuvers needs to become second nature.

RIVER BENDS

As rivers flow around sharp bends, the force of the current usually concentrates, pushing water into the outside bank of the bend. It often picks up speed there and can build up compression waves due to a more restricted and concentrated flow. Water that's squeezed in a narrow, swift channel wants to go somewhere. It tends to go up, building into taller waves, which are ultimately held in check by gravity (When that compressed water suddenly gets the chance to spread back out laterally, it can create strong whirlpools in big side eddies or behind boulders.) Some river waves exceed 20 feet. As water sprawls across the tailout of a river beyond the bend, it tends to spread out and flatten as gravity smears it across a widened bed.

As the water rushes around the outside bend, it both erodes it and tends to lodge some boulders and logs there. The bank along an outside bend is often steep. Boulders get exposed or rolled into place there, either from being pushed by water and ice over the years or from rolling down the eroded hillside. In either case, it's not unusual to find the outside of a bend littered with boulders, rocks, and perhaps a log or two. The inside bend, on the other hand, is usually composed of finer sands, gravel, or cobble. The eddy there, known as the eye of the pool, is slower and circulates horizontally, allowing finer silts and sands to drop out of the current (and allowing trout to hold there). The heavy currents on the swifter banks keep those silts

MANEUVERING AROUND SHARP RIVER BENDS

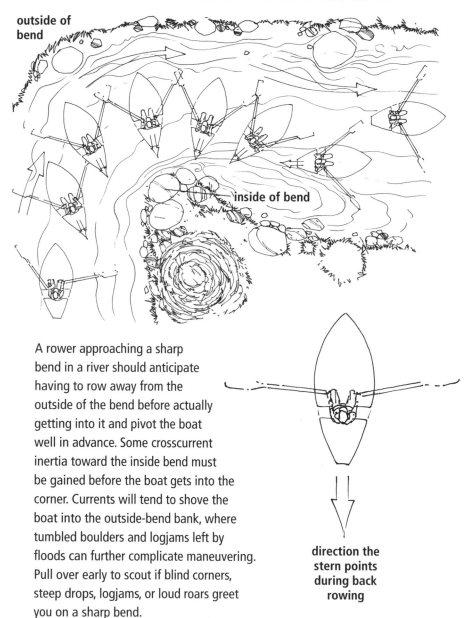

outside of bend

inside of bend

A rower approaching a sharp bend in a river should anticipate having to row away from the outside of the bend before actually getting into it and pivot the boat well in advance. Some crosscurrent inertia toward the inside bend must be gained before the boat gets into the corner. Currents will tend to shove the boat into the outside-bend bank, where tumbled boulders and logjams left by floods can further complicate maneuvering. Pull over early to scout if blind corners, steep drops, logjams, or loud roars greet you on a sharp bend.

direction the stern points during back rowing

moving, allowing only heavy rocks to settle and not get pushed any farther downstream—until the next ice jam or flood.

Because the current can be expected to push a boat toward the outside bend, you'll want to angle the stern *crosscurrent* a bit, aiming it toward the inside bend of the river before you actually get into the corner. River currents are not always parallel with the banks, so be alert to the direction of the current, not just to the banks. You also need to begin making stronger oar strokes to get some back-ferrying momentum built up before entering the corner itself. Once you have a back-rowing head of steam, the proper back-ferrying angle, and correct entry setup, negotiating bends becomes easier. There can be big boulders to dodge, both in the chute and along the steeper, swifter bank. Be alert for these. Rocks, holes, and logjams can all be found along sharp bends. They require an extra level of awareness and preparedness in order to make quick decisions and take evasive action.

Beginners get into trouble when they let themselves be pushed too far into the outside bend before beginning to back away from it. If nothing else, this tends to cut into the fishing potential if the boat is shoved right up against a bank. The bankside oar can be rendered useless by the shore's proximity until the boat is pivoted into the proper ferrying angle to get away from it. This will be harder, because the full force of the current is driving the boat into the bank. Collisions with boulders and logs are common, too, when beginners fail to ferry away from a corner before getting right into it. These are prime locations to wrap a boat or flip in a hole. Damage can be done to boats, and equipment can be lost when the craft side-slams even minor rocks or logs.

If you recall the discussion of the crawl stroke in Chapter 2, it, too, can be used to round corners if they're not too demanding. I usually use a combination of the backstroke and the crawl when rounding corners, endeavoring to keep a smooth

There are many times when you'll want to pull the boat over and stop, both to scout difficult runs and to fish pools just downstream before floating over them.

rowing pace and even track so anglers aren't jostled and can capitalize on this fish-producing zone. If your float time allows, it's a good idea to row around the bend, pull over, anchor or tie off a little way down the run, and come back upstream to wade-fish the eye of the pool, eddy line, and perhaps systematically nymph the drop-off leading into them. If you can reach the far side, it's usually sprinkled with fish-holding pockets among the larger rocks found there and is well worth pursuing. It could be more productive to drop an angler off on that side at the tail of the run and then go anchor on the other side and let the second angler go up the inside bend. In that way, both sides as well as the middle of the river are covered most thoroughly.

READING AND CLEARING RAPIDS
Although running technical whitewater is beyond the scope of this book, it does every boater good to get some whitewater

experience to hone rowing skills. There are plenty of great fishing rivers with well-known rapids. Most rapids are an intensification of water speed, river drop, channelization, sharp turns, and boulder congestion. The ability to read water, set up, make quick decisions, and carry them out becomes critical in whitewater. Turbulence and waves can make getting a good oar plant trickier at times. The need for pivot turns and power back ferries can come fast and furiously. There can be holes that eat boats in a blink of an eye. The basic required maneuvers are the same, but the more powerful water pushes you harder, testing your skills and strength. A couple of missed oar strokes due to water turbulence or a faulty read can end in a collision, spill, or wrap.

Types of rapids vary, largely due to the bedrock formations rivers flow through, in addition to the residual effects of landslides, which drop some huge boulders into rivers along steeply eroded slopes. Any combination of elements can be found. Some rivers tend to have fairly straightforward pool-drop run sequences. A few have boulder gardens and big standing waves for miles on end. The latter aren't run for fishing much but are mostly whitewater playgrounds (though many do have good fishing at low flows). Because we're most interested in fishing applications and generally mellower rivers, we'll discuss some of these added hazards only briefly.

Rock or Boulder Gardens

"Rock garden" is a whitewater term for a boulder-studded reach of river. Many are caused by rock slides off steep hillsides or avalanche chutes. Over the centuries (and one really does float through time, geologically speaking, on a river), accumulated rock slides can fill a section of river with big boulders. These occur mostly on outside bends of the river, where a steep bank continually erodes. These areas create challenging runs, the kind whitewater enthusiasts thrive on. Adrenaline rushes are as addictive for them as rising trout for fishermen. There are many famous rapids that were caused by rock slides. Avalanches, heavy rain and erosion, floods, ice jams, and earthquakes all can create and rearrange rapids.

Many boulder gardens call for scouting. A deep roar and unclear channel should lead you to the bank. Beach the boat well upstream of the rapid, so that upon reembarking you have the rowing room to set up properly anywhere across the river. After beaching, crew members should walk downstream to explore and memorize the different possible rowing routes. The best route is chosen, and its landmarks noted. Things will look a lot different once you are out in the water, however. Sometimes, in a technical piece of water, the boatman might opt to take the boat through alone. Reducing the human weight by several hundred pounds makes it easier to row. On the other hand, a heavier boat doesn't usually flip as easily, especially if everyone on board knows how to use their weight as ballast. There might be party members who physically wouldn't be up to any mishaps or a nasty swim through the rapids. Some people have an undeniable fear of big churning water, too. Such party members will feel a lot safer walking around threatening rapids. No amount of cajoling will have much effect on this state of mind, though going through a progression of river trips, from easy to moderate and finally to challenging, can lessen the fear of water, along with a good understanding of how water acts and how to deal with it. There are quite a few people who love to fish yet have a fear of moving water.

In any case, after scouting the rapid, tighten life jackets, lash down equipment, and make sure the crew is prepared for any eventuality. Having identified the best route, the rower tries to memorize the boulder sequence and his upcoming maneuvers, much like a downhill skier memorizes his course. Knowing your route ahead of time is of great advantage when you need to make a split-second decision, and surging currents

VARIOUS HAZARDS AND RAPIDS

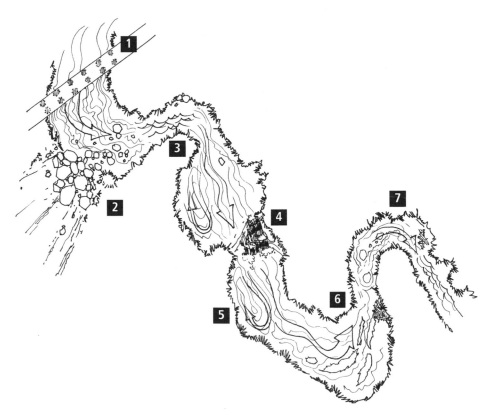

1. Bridge pilings with narrow slots and low bridges.
2. Boulder gardens, often caused by landslides off steep hillsides.
3. Large compression waves caused by a narrowing chute intensified by a steeper drop. Side curlers rolling off cliff walls and serious holes are likely, too. Powerhouse whirlpools can occur when the water has a chance to spread back out. This is a typical gorge scenario.
4. Ledge drops and man-made diversion dams can create bad holes.
5. Strong whirlpools where rivers widen are particularly strong in high water.
6. Narrow, congested channels in island systems. Watch for logjams.
7. Blind corners can lead into rapids and logjams. If in doubt, scout!

make some oar strokes a lot less effective than you hoped they'd be.

Once you enter the rapid, maneuver with strong back-strokes—never forward ones. The crawl stroke isn't strong enough for big-water work; you will likely need to make quick pivots and power ferries, strong backstrokes you lean into at 30- to 45-degree angles across the current. Eddies behind big boulders can be used to help slow the boat down and cross over to different current lanes. Don't pull in too closely and get sucked back up into a hole. Big holes are to be feared and avoided, if at all possible. If you are headed for one (and there are plenty of cases where big holes are unavoidable), increase your downstream speed in hopes of blasting through it. If you're sucked back into it, remain alert and use your body weight to counteract flips. You may at times have to spin the boat completely around in a tight maneuver between boulders. I have fun doing this occasionally in a calculated rock-squeezing fashion, using the eddies behind to help suck me in and spin back around. Naturally, anglers should have their fly lines in when performing such maneuvers. A skilled crew, though, can have fun fishing their way through a rapid if it is not overwhelming. Such stretches don't see much fishing pressure. Pockets will need to be covered fast, but the fish can be just as fast at grabbing your fly. Swift-water rivers often breed gung-ho trout.

You may encounter boulder gardens that are either too narrow to even squeeze a boat through or so powerful that your better judgment elects not to run them. In these cases you must either portage your boat and equipment around the rapid or line through. To line a boat, tie long ropes to the bow and stern and walk along the shore, holding tightly to the ropes to lead the empty craft along the edge of the rapids. A boat minus its human cargo weight can often be slid over shallow spots you couldn't otherwise float through. In heavy-water spots, you might want to snub the boat, or wrap a rope around a rock or tree on shore before letting the boat proceed. The added friction of the rope around the rock or tree slows the boat's progress, giving you greater control and lessening the chance that you'll be pulled into the water. Boulder gardens and rapids often call for intelligent decisions and contingency plans.

Many of the rock gardens I encounter in midsummer have lots of boulders but not very powerful flows. Fishing is good in these places. Row here as smoothly as possible, putting anglers in the best position you can. The crawl stroke again becomes a most useful ploy, reducing excess pivot turns and ferries to minimums. You still have to be cautious, though. It's possible to wrap boats around rocks in fairly insignificant flows.

Standing Waves

Ocean waves move, rolling in toward the coast. River waves stay relatively still—the water moves through them. In rapids, these are often called standing waves. They're usually caused by the narrowing of a river channel or the concentration of an accelerating current down a chute. River waves are sometimes referred to as "compression waves."

On smaller scales, there's not much to worry about. Many chutes with smaller standing waves are deep, with few or no rocks to dodge. Always be alert, though, because boulders or logs could still be hidden within. When waves start getting more than 3 or 4 feet high, it's time to be on your toes. Here, too, many chutes with compression waves are deep and have no obstacles to dodge. There are, however, many chutes and rapids with big waves that are also boulder-studded or have sudden ledge drops. Seeing obstacles ahead becomes more difficult, because tall waves obscure your forward view. When down in the trough between two waves, you might not be able to see anything except the top of the next wave. It's when your boat rides the crests of waves that you want to scan ahead for hidden boulders, ledges, and killer holes. In a deep, straight-

Standing waves form in rivers where there are big drops or constricted currents. Waves of 2 to 10 feet are common in some locations. An inverted V slot, as seen in this picture, often shows the most straightforward way through. Big standing waves might be easily negotiated, but they can also hide perils just downstream, such as killer holes.

forward chute, the waves will be regularly spaced and similar in height. The boat trip through will be like a roller coaster ride. In a more complex rapid, irregular, extra-tall, and back-curling waves, side curlers, and sudden flat spots in the channel ahead can indicate the presence of boulders, ledges, logs, and holes. You might even need to stand up in your boat briefly to get a better view over the waves and chart your course. Again, you may want to scout any rapid in question before committing to run it. You'll want to be ready to make instant decisions, quick pivot turns, and powerful backstrokes.

Even if you give a boulder a glancing blow, the water that heaves off its upstream side will tend to shove your boat away from it at the last second. During a last-ditch evasion, this might send you into a spin from which you'll quickly need to right yourself. In big water, back-curling waves breaking off a large boulder can be big enough to flip boats that go into them sideways. Pay attention to wave height and turbulence. Pivot and back-row when you can, but spin your boat nose-first into big back curlers, waves, and holes when the threat of a flip is real. You often have to make split-second changes, ferrying in one direction, then having to spin your bow into big side curlers the next moment, and then reestablishing your original ferry angle just as quickly.

Bigger waves are cause for greater concern. River waves of 6 feet in height are quite common. Ten- to 15-foot waves can be found on many whitewater rivers and on some popular fishing rivers in flood. There are even monster waves of 15 to 30 feet on a few waters.

When waves get beyond a certain height, they often form back curlers, similar in look to those breaking on an ocean beach. These can be turbulent enough to flip boats that go into them sideways, or at least they will fill them with a lot of water. Small rafts can even surf on giant waves like kayaks, and they can slide back down the wave into the trough if the wave is tall enough and the raft's forward motion is stalled. The back-curling wave can then keep breaking onto the boat, flushing it with water. Boats half full of water weigh thousands of pounds. Rowing that kind of additional weight around doesn't get you very far! This is one reason self-bailing rafts (and even drift boats) have become popular in whitewater circles. Rafts filled with water are largely at the river's mercy. A boater's control of them is minimal.

With the right bottom configuration or channelization, it's easy for big waves to evolve into holes. A series of big standing waves with back curlers might drop over just a bit of a ledge or big boulder, which suddenly confronts you with a flip-worthy hole.

The trick is to hit big back-curling waves nose-on. Avoid getting into them sideways. You might need to repeatedly pivot the boat, both for maneuvering and to hit big waves nose-on. The nature of compression waves means they often break at angles, coming from both sides of the river. You might have to swing your nose into the crest of each really big wave, just at the last second—first right, then left, back right, and so on. Sometimes maneuvering becomes an absolute must. Consequently, some big waves have to be broadsided to some degree. This is another case where using human cargo as ballast can be important. If a big wave starts to flip your boat over sideways, your crew needs to throw their body weight into the high side in an attempt to knock it back down and avoid a flip. This becomes something like throwing a football body block in extreme cases. It's not unusual to find yourself occasionally thrown to the floor of the boat. It is necessary to stay aware of the boat's position in the water and to adjust the human ballast in order to keep the craft upright. Extreme case, yes. But it does happen on some trout and steelhead rivers.

In steep-walled canyons and along some sharp river bends, big waves can break as they pile up against the banks. Such waves can be irregular and surging, angling off the walls at about 45-degree angles. Many such waves can be totally avoided with the proper setup and advance back ferrying. The current, though, will be trying to shove you into the wall. If you let the river push you too far, you'll have to both angle your boat sharply away from the outside bend wall and pivot the bow of your boat to hit big back curlers head-on. You might have to maneuver and back-row like mad in the troughs of the waves and swing the nose back around for every big breaking crest. It's possible for the water to shove a poorly controlled craft right into the wall, where an oar can be incapacitated or broken. This leaves you temporarily at the river's mercy, and some big waves, boulders, and holes are likely to be just down-

SIDE CURLERS

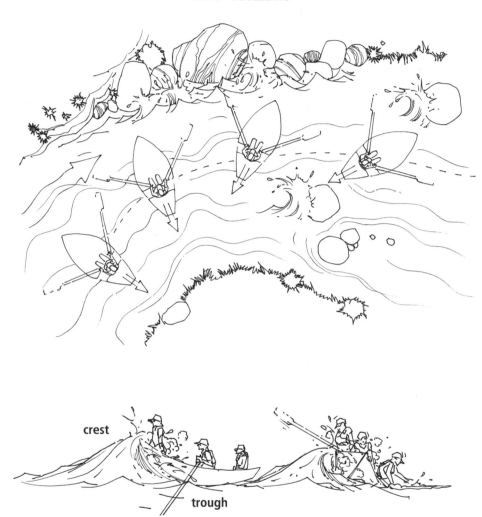

crest

trough

Big side curlers rolling off cliff walls and boulders can flip small fishing craft. Avoid them when possible or hit them bow-first, not sideways. Sometimes a serious evasive rowing maneuver may make it necessary to broadside a big back curler or hole. If so, use your human ballast to counteract any boat-flipping tendencies, and row like mad.

stream! This is a typical flip scenario. Early recognition, setup, and preliminary back-ferrying momentum are the keys to staying out of trouble here.

Once you get the feel of running more challenging water and get some whitewater experience, you'll have a lot of fun at the oars. A mix of good fishing with some stretches of moderate whitewater makes for an enjoyable day. The diversity keeps your mind alert as you drift through beautiful canyons and valleys. The sights, sounds, and river-scented breezes (which can be caused by moving water) combine to make a special chemistry craved by all river addicts.

Swimming and Self-Rescue in Rapids
The time-honored method of swimming through a rapid, rock garden, or other area of swift water depends upon a high-quality, type 5 life jacket and the defensive positioning of the backstroke. Type 5 life jackets (a government standard) are highly buoyant, with a collar that theoretically keeps the wearer's head above water, even if the wearer is unconscious. Consider the term "whitewater." It's rushing, tumbling water that appears white because it's infused with air bubbles. The whiter it is, the more air is churned into it, and the less you float. Your buoyancy goes down as air infusion goes up, even with a life jacket. Add to this the down-pulling currents of a hole, crashing back curler, or whirlpool, and the need for a life jacket becomes obvious. No knowledgeable boater, even the best, thinks of running a whitewater stretch without a life jacket.

On the whole, anglers tend not to wear life jackets because they restrict movement. Anglers wear fishing vests and usually have a degree of faith in their guide or boatman. However, life jackets are required aboard most watercraft by law in most states. Anglers should put them on whenever facing water they

SWIMMING IN RAPIDS

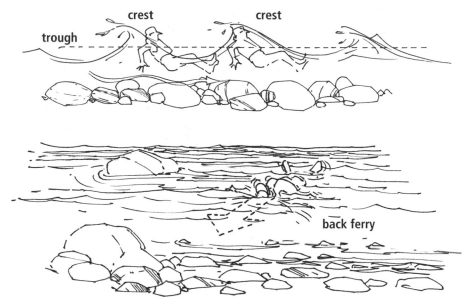

If you do get washed out of a boat in heavy water, immediately assume a backstroking position, assess your situation, and back ferry toward the boat or nearest safe shore. Use your feet and hands to fend off boulders. Don't try to stand up until you've reached shallow waters. Keep your feet near the surface. When going through big waves, expect your head to go under the water in the crests. Keep your eyes open and your mind alert. Breathe in the troughs when your head resurfaces. Hold your breath in the crests, holes, and whenever you see that you're about to go under. Always wear a life jacket in strong water.

wouldn't feel comfortable swimming through, especially if their rower is a novice.

The swimming backstroke position confers three advantages: The swimmer can see where he is headed downstream; he can use feet and hands to fend off rocks; at the same time, he can backstroke toward shore, using a 45-degree ferrying angle that he'd use if rowing. An angler who gets washed or dumped out of a boat can usually just swim back to it unless separated from the boat by swirling whirlpools and currents. It's decidedly tougher to reenter a boat when wearing a life jacket, though, especially if you are also encumbered by waders, a jacket, and what have you. It can be necessary for the rest of the crew to drag a swimmer back on board while also navigating tricky water. Any swimmer hanging on to the outside of a boat that's still going through rough water should avoid being on the downstream end or side of the boat, where a collision with a rock could put the swimmer between the two.

Don't try to stand up in swift, boulder-studded water. There's a chance your feet can get stuck between rocks and wedged there. If this happens, the current will knock you over. With an anchored foot, you'll be flattened by the river and very possibly shoved underwater. Drownings, even of people wearing high-quality life jackets, happen this way from time to time. Instead of trying to stand once you've fallen in, immediately assume the backstroke position, keeping your feet near the water surface. Look for the boat or nearest safe bank, and start backstroking there at a ferrying angle. Don't stand up until you reach slower shallow water, where getting your foot snagged would be unlikely.

An angler wearing waders and no life jacket faces a more serious swim. If the waders are baggy at all, they'll balloon out a bit when the wearer backstrokes against the current, causing noticeable and unwanted drag. Swim more sideways to the current or a little down and across in this case, because then the current will have less effect on your waders. Well-tailored waders and a wading belt are big pluses when swimming. Today's lighter-weight breathable waders pose less of a threat, yet will still bog down swimming to some degree. Do keep your eyes open, too. Pick a swimming route and prepare to use your feet and hands to fend off rocks while backstroking. A pillow surrounds rocks, caused by the water moving around them. It will usually lessen any physical impact with the rocks. Tightly clustered boulders act like sieves, however, and should be avoided if possible.

When you are swimming through big waves, expect your head to go underwater through the crest of each wave. It will reemerge once you're heading down into the next trough. It's very important to keep your eyes open so that you know when to breathe and where to swim. There are many turbulences that will submerge your head at times, even if you are wearing the best life jacket. Wave crests and breakers, holes, and whirlpools can all temporarily push or suck you under. You must see opportunities to breathe or hold your breath as long as necessary. If you don't keep your eyes open and your mind alert, you'll be at much greater risk. Try not to panic if you fall in the river. Immediately sum up your position and the boat's position, formulate a plan of self-rescue, and implement it using the backstroke.

If you've never fallen into ice-cold water, be aware of its effects. First, it will make you gasp for breath, sometimes uncontrollably. Not being able to choose moments of breathing when swimming through rough water is an added danger. You can become numb and half-paralyzed in a very short period of time, sometimes even less than a minute. The better the shape you're in (with little body fat), the quicker you can be affected by the cold. Soon you'll have a hard time effectively swimming or grabbing onto bankside rocks to save yourself. Before very long, your thinking will become disoriented; you won't even care much about what's going on. Hypothermia sets in fast. This is a real danger in the early season, when rivers can be high and icy cold. Late-season trips carry the hypothermia threat, too, though most rivers are low and clear then. People even get hypothermia in midsummer, during cold windstorms and rainstorms. Some rivers below big dams never warm up much.

Early and late in the season, extricating yourself from the river doesn't end your troubles, because cold air temperatures and wind only heighten the hypothermic effect. A fire could be an absolute necessity, along with a change of clothes. This is one reason polypropylene and fleece clothes are so popular with floaters and anglers. The water-repelling properties of polypropylene and some newer synthetics make them a top insulating choice. You can wring and whip most of the water from a synthetic garment, and it will feel almost dry. Don't get them too close to the fire, though—they can melt.

If you are unable to get a fire going after a cold-water, cold-weather spill, get off the river as fast as you can: Head for the nearest warm environment. Ultimately, a victim of severe hypothermia can be kept alive by the age-old method whereby all party members strip off their clothes and huddle tightly around the hypothermic party member in whatever they can wrap around themselves for insulation. Body heat can save the life of a victim of hypothermia in extreme cases.

WHIRLPOOLS

Whirlpools occur where a powerful concentrated water flow opens into a suddenly widened riverbed. They also occur behind boulders, bridge abutments, and the like that block strong current flows. Most whirlpools on trout rivers aren't powerful enough to flip or suck under drift boats or rafts. There are some on powerful steelhead and whitewater rivers that can, though, and canoes and smaller craft are much more at risk.

The rapid direction change of the current at the center of a whirlpool can have an effect similar to a hole. One side will be shoved under as the boat abruptly swings around. Awareness and the use of human ballast are necessary, along with a continued attempt to avoid the heart of the whirlpool. Most whirlpools can be avoided, but beginning rowers sometimes find themselves in one because of lack of attention or knowledge.

Almost every year, someone drowns on the Missouri near where I live, a stretch of river that's big in volume but flat. Even though it's a relatively mellow flat-surfaced river, some of its whirlpools at higher water levels are very strong. When canoes are flipped, some people inadvertently swim into the whirlpools. These whirlpools will jerk a drift boat around but will rarely flip one. I have been on more-powerful rivers where the difference between the center of the whirlpool and its outer edges is several feet or more. I've experienced one that sucked the front end of a big 16-foot raft underwater! It's hard to row out of big whirlpools, and even more difficult to swim through them. Keep your eyes open and breathe when you can. You will come out before long, but it can seem a long time when you're underwater.

The most turbulent situations occur where a heavy current runs by a boulder, cliff edge, or bridge abutment. The difference in current speed between the downstream main current flow and that of the water running upstream behind the impediment can be extreme. There can even be an altitude difference between the two. Pulling into a whirlpooling eddy right behind a boulder can upset a drift boat. Pulling back into the main current from right behind one can be even worse. Instead, pull in behind obstacles a little farther downstream, where the current difference isn't so extreme. The same goes for pulling out into the main current from behind a river-blocking feature: Drop downstream a bit before reentering a heavy current.

EFFECTS OF THE ELEMENTS

Sun, wind, rain, snow, cold, and heat all influence the river in subtle to catastrophic ways. Wind, for example, is a rowing obstacle that you might not initially think of. Its effect on rafts and drift boats is great, though, because their surface area is large enough to be pushed by the wind. Drift boats are especially bad in this respect. The high sides and bottom curvature (rocker) that allow them to maneuver and handle rough water so well also mean that they blow like a leaf across the surface. This can be very disconcerting to a novice rower. A boatman might have to row like mad to keep his boat from getting slammed into the bank by a crosswind on even a lazy, straight stretch of river that's normally a no-brainer. Rowing in the wind can take more strength and endurance than running rapids, for the wind is often unrelenting. A downstream gale will shove you down the river faster than you want to go unless a rather brutal measure of back rowing is kept up every second. (This is particularly rough on the palms of your hands!) An upstream blow can at times make downstream progress almost impossible. I have been in spots where even back-rowing as hard as I could in the strongest current produced no downstream headway. We ended up walking the boat downstream.

There are landscapes that concentrate wind, and landscapes that block it. I know a spot on a canyon river where the wind tunnel effect is so pronounced that grass clumps on one bank will be divided, with each half blown in opposite directions, just like parted hair! Some big-river valleys, like the Yellowstone, are known for their afternoon winds. Other, smaller rivers have a greater degree of wind block. Across the Rocky Mountain West, though, wind is a daily reality. Where I guide, wind is the biggest rowing obstacle. Water-related obstacles rate a distant second.

On the whole, crosswinds are the worst to row in. You often have to go down the river sideways, with your stern to the wind rather than against the current. You'll be rowing against a combination of the two. Fly fishers might not be having much fun at this point either: The chances of hooking each other with casts led astray by the wind go up with every gust.

Besides actually getting blown into banks, shallows, rocks, or what have you, beginners must be aware of oar dig, as discussed in Chapter 2. Don't allow the boat to get blown along at

On windy days, you might want to pull over along lee shores for some easier casting. Trout don't like to rise routinely in the wind, so wind-free slicks might be the only places you'll see them.

a high speed sideways and then deeply dig your downwind oar. You'll find yourself getting unintentionally blown into some shallow areas, too, where the boat will start banging the streambed and your oars will have little grab or will get jammed into the bottom. What's important is to constantly maintain control and never let the boat get too much out of hand, especially if you are coming into a challenging bit of water.

On rivers that call for some trick maneuvering, wind can buffet you at inopportune moments, interfering at the last second with your setup and subsequent rowing route. An extra level of attention and physical effort may be necessary.

You can learn to set up for wind gusts just as you would for other obstacles. You can actually see and hear wind gusts coming. Windblown water and waving grasses and trees let you know that a sudden blast is about to pound you. Wind direction is somewhat constant, so when you see a gust coming, position the boat to battle the wind as needed, swinging your stern into it, and lay on some heavy preliminary oar strokes. Look for the more sheltered, or lee, side of the river to float down. You might want to concentrate on wind-free areas by pulling over to anchor, wade-fishing them thoroughly. Rising trout don't like wind either. Wind-free slicks along protected banks might be the only places you'll find steadily rising fish. Ultimately, if most of the time you fish one or two favorite pieces of water whose rowing requirements aren't too challenging, you might want to buy a boat that has good wind-rowing properties above all else. We'll look at this more closely in Chapter 6.

Thunderstorms can present some extreme experiences. When I see those big, nasty clouds roll in too closely, I start looking for cover. The abundant willows where I guide are great to take cover in. They're low, dense, and unlikely to be struck by lightning, while at the same time they block most wind, rain, and hail. Our thunderstorms don't last very long. It's their initial impact and potential wind speeds that are so menacing. I'll hang near some willows as a storm draws near, take cover when it hits, then get down the river a bit for the good fishing that often materializes when clouds and cool, moist weather kick in. Should another thunderhead be rolling in, I'll be thinking of the next willow grove and calculating how long I need to get there.

Lightning in mountain valleys seems to stay up pretty high, usually hitting somewhere on the upper half of the slopes. I don't worry about getting struck by lightning as much on mountain rivers, though I do look for low, thick willows as cover. Prairie rivers are another matter. Lightning hits low and often. Winds are particularly fierce. The hail pummels. Here, there might be no willows, only old and crumbling cottonwood groves. These are lousy places to take cover because they're brittle and drop big limbs with regularity in big blows. Lightning strikes are distinct possibilities here, too. It's better to seek whatever low, dense brush you can find to weather a storm, perhaps following deer tracks a little way up a protected coulee. Wide rivers do pose lightning threats. A boat was struck on the Missouri River a few years back.

In wind storms, you also need to be careful of anchoring your boat. Enough wind will cause a boat to drag its anchor, especially if the anchor is on a short length of rope. A longer length of rope allows the anchor a better bite in the streambed. The rope angle, when it's long, produces less pressure on the anchor.

Here's an all too common thunderstorm scenario: A fishing party sees, smells, hears, and feels a big thunderhead rolling toward them. All agree it would be best to take cover. The party drops anchor near the bank, huddling in a storm-tight grotto. Feeling pretty secure, they might even light up a good cigar and settle in to watch the show. Powerful winds start hitting, dust flies, and the first rain and hail start pelting down. The boat is swinging on its rope. The wind increases, trees lean, thunder booms. Suddenly, the boat starts towing the anchor out across the river—being anchored on too short a rope allowed the boat to drag it more easily. The deeper the water the boat blows out to, the less hold the anchor has. Eventually, the boat reaches water that's deep enough that the anchor no longer touches the bottom, and off it goes downstream. Its owner scrambles to reach it in time, but it all happened so fast that he's last seen running downstream, splashing through the shallows downriver in hopes of retrieving his craft. Chances are it'll end up on the other side. He'll need to flag a boat ride to find it.

When a big storm approaches I pull my drift boat halfway up the bank so it won't blow around, release a long length of anchor rope, and wedge the anchor way up on dry land. If there is a tree nearby, I'll wrap the rope around it a couple of times for security. You could as easily anchor your boat in shallow water with its rope fully extended, but the boat can start swinging around on the long rope and is likely to repeatedly bang into stream-edge rocks, chipping the hull. You can also use a heavier anchor—35 pounds should do it. Most drift boats in my area favor 30-pound anchors. If you get too heavy an anchor, pulling it in throughout the day will be a real chore, perhaps more work than it's worth (though there are pulley systems that reduce the effort).

If I have to park along a very steep, rocky bank to sit out a storm, I'll usually stay with the boat the whole time, hail and all, to hold it and keep it from bashing itself against the rocks. This is one of those acts of love that wooden-boat owners are likely to display to preserve the finish of their hand-built crafts.

Many rafts don't have an anchor system at all, and some owners don't even carry anchors. I've had to transport a few rafters who pulled their boat too lightly up the shore, only to have it blow away. Very cheap light rafts can even become airborne. I saw one blow across the wide Missouri once and get pinned up in some cliffs on the other side! The owners, who mistakenly left the raft alone on the bank to get their car, couldn't believe their plight! Always carry an anchor or a tie-down rope at least 25 feet long. Trees don't always grow down to the edge of the water along some floodplain rivers. Raft owners need rope to make sure they can secure their boat in wind, especially if it's left alone.

Although wind on the whole is no friend of an oarsman, it does have a few benefits. It blows hoppers, terrestrial insects, and damselflies into the river, attracting larger trout. Light wind can ripple the water just enough to make trout less picky and spooky, because their vision becomes somewhat obscured. You

Late summer hopper fishing can be good on windy days. Brown grass keeps hoppers moving in search of better food supplies, and many get blown into the river.

can often get away with slightly larger flies and slightly heavier tippet in a light to medium wind chop. On those searing summer days, a little breeze feels good, but only a little! Wind also chases some anglers off the river, which can give you a little more solitude.

Glare

Sunshine is another one of those less-tangible river obstacles that you might not consider unless you happen to be floating down a west-flowing river into a brilliant sunset. The sun can be blinding if it's in the wrong quarter. There's not much you can do about it besides the usual hat and polarized sunglasses. On choppy rivers with a few rock gardens thrown in, the glare off waves and water droplets is too much to see through. I've

A steep or wooded bank blocks sky reflection, making it easier to spot fish beneath the surface. Look patiently for fish shapes, shadows they cast on the bottom, and for movement that gives them away.

found this to be the case on parts of Montana's Blackfoot River where it flows directly west.

If your eyes are particularly sensitive, you might want to consider the direction a river flows and the hours you fish it. Avoid east-flowing rivers at sunrise and west-flowing ones toward dusk. You might even choose to fish on overcast days, which often produce better fishing anyway. Make sure you have a hat and sunglasses on hand to combat daylong glare, which is hard on the eyes.

When it comes to ease of viewing and especially spotting rising fish and trout *under* the water, it's best to use a steep, wooded bank as a viewing backdrop. This eliminates a lot of glare. Gaining ideal viewing positions can add up to more fish caught. In the float-fishing game, spotting fish is just as important as avoiding river obstacles.

MAN-MADE HAZARDS

Although diversion dams top the list of hazardous man-made obstructions, there are a few others to be concerned with as well. Barbed-wire fences are stretched across some smaller rivers to keep cattle confined to their owners' properties. Some fish and game departments have designed "floater's gates" and installed them in place of barbed-wire fences. These curtainlike contraptions made of PVC pipe allow floaters to glide through them while psychologically detaining cattle, whose creative instincts for revolution and escape seem genetically limited.

Barbed-wire fences can be low and tight, requiring one or two party members to go out ahead of the boat and lift the fence strands before the boat tries to pass underneath it. Don't try to float up to a fence and lift it from the boat. If the fence can't be lifted high enough, the boat can get pinned by the force of the current and punctured. People, too, are easily sliced by the barbs. Ultimately, it helps to keep some combination wire snips–needlenose pliers on board, plus a little length of wire or cord, especially if you think you might encounter fences. If you have to cut a strand or two to get by, you can then repair the fence. Many landowners are already touchy enough about having people float through their property without having their cattle escape, too. These tools also come in handy for other repairs.

Irrigation canals pose potential problems on some rivers. They can head off a river and appear to be just another side channel. After getting down one a little way, you'll probably run into a small dam or gate. Now, having realized your dilemma, you have to pull your boat back upstream to the main channel again, which isn't always an easy task. Many western hay meadows are flood-irrigated from these canals, which breed hordes of blood-sucking mosquitoes. I've heard a few tales of woe about dragging boats back up out of irrigation canals while swatting madly and being devoured by mosquitoes. Naturally, such adventures in floating are most likely to happen on balmy summer days, when the chosen attire is shorts and wading sandals.

Bridge pilings and low bridges are common hazards, too. Some are tight squeezes in strong currents and call for controlled rowing. High water makes some low bridges impassable. This makes their discovery by an unsuspecting party rather critical, necessitating a tedious portage. On some rivers, there are old pilings that are just barely submerged and capable of ripping rafts. Old car bodies once used to brace eroding banks, fence posts, and other farm debris are common in riverbeds and feature sharp boat-piercing metal. You also have to watch for and row around sunken trees and waterlogged limbs. River channels can completely change after floods and ice jams, presenting new obstacles, both natural and man-made.

Float fishers should be able to learn of most river hazards in advance from modern floaters' maps, books, and advice from local fish and game departments and fishing shops. Float fishers should be otherwise alert and able to recognize different dangers and know how to row or portage around them. Once safety, knowledge, and rowing skills are ingrained, the fishing potential gets better and better.

4

Rowing Strategies for Anglers

A rowboat is an effective fishing tool only when the boatman understands fish behavior and rows for the angler's advantage. Just being in a boat doesn't guarantee better fishing. Indeed, it can be a detriment if it's not properly controlled, if the boat whisks by hot spots rather than slowing or stopping by them. Let's examine several facets of float fishing with a goal of improving your catch rate.

THINKING LIKE A TROUT

Being a successful trout fisher, a really successful one, hinges on understanding trout behavior—their needs, moods, feeding habits, fears, and seasonal peculiarities (ditto for salmon, steelhead, and smallmouth). From a float-fishing perspective, knowing where trout hold in a river is the highest priority. Being able to cast well and accurately and being able to control line drag once the fly is on the water rates a close second. Knowing what local trout are eating is important, but even generalized patterns will catch fish if casts and line control are good. It's easier to find out what the current hatches are than it is to learn to cast and fish well. Finally, you might need certain equipment to

Thinking like a trout will up your catch rate. Look at bottom contours, foam lines, current seams, eddies, bank cover, and other potential hot zones. Analyze them before you get to them, and cast ahead of the boat with a reach cast. If two people are fishing, they should cover different zones.

routinely catch fish. For instance, late-spring conditions can produce rising muddy waters where only a well-sunk stonefly nymph might bring regular success. If you don't have the weighted nymphs and weighting system to get line, leader, and fly near the bottom, you won't catch the fish.

Trout have few immediate needs in life: eat, survive, spawn. Although they need moving water and its conveyance of food, trout don't want too much of a good thing. They hold in places where moderated currents prevail, a good food supply is delivered, and safety is close at hand. Most fish will be off to the sides of the main currents, or under them along the bottom.

The rower's mind is alert to the trout's needs. He positions anglers where they can most effectively fish for trout—within casting range and where the best line control can be exerted so that drag is minimized. He must also position the boat so it's least likely to be seen by the fish. It's an added advantage if the boat can be rowed in place or anchored in this optimal position as long as necessary to achieve success. In other cases, when no particular hot spots are on hand, just slowing the boat down and keeping it a constant distance from the target bank or water will be the top rowing priority. There will be places where it's best to pull over and wade-fish for optimal results.

Perhaps the best way to look at some of the trout's favorite hangouts is to take a hypothetical stretch of river and analyze various water types one at a time. Our medium-to-large proto-type river will allow us to explore most situations found on a variety of trout rivers. Our conclusions might also be applied to smallmouth bass and other species. Stream character, fish behavior, and hatches vary from river to river, though, even in the same geographic area and with the same species of fish.

The rower positions the angler at the best location and angle for success. Rowers not only navigate safely, they understand the fisherman's casting limitations and know what casting angle is most likely to succeed in a certain circumstance. They endeavor to hold the boat in just that spot.

Float-fishing for trout can be a series of problem-solving experiences, and rowing anglers keep their minds open and attentive to such idiosyncrasies.

Before starting down the river, let's consider a few things. Fish could be on either side of the river almost anywhere along our route, or down the middle. The crew will naturally want to choose the side with the best concentrations of fish and the most well-defined trout-holding water. On a small river, each caster could take a side. On big rivers, you'll have to choose one side or the other. And although the most obvious and well-defined trout spots can be easy enough to figure out, the subtler holding waters will be of great interest, too. There might already be anglers at many of the obvious places. Understanding the second-best choices, therefore, can be important, and on many occasions it's those spots that will make a day. Many small hot spots in a river may hold only a fish or two, and broad midriver zones are well populated. Added up over the course of a day's fishing, this can tally a good percentage of the catch.

Position 1

Our trip finds us floating down the long belly of a straight stretch of river (refer to the illustration), heading toward the tailout. Commonly, one side will be a little bit steeper, deeper, and swifter than the other (usually this is the outside bank leading down from the previous bend in the river). This is our A side. The opposite side will be a little shallower and slower paced.

The A side is the deeper of the two, and chances are there might be an undercut bank, fallen chunks of eroded turf, and perhaps a big rock or log or two, all creating eddying fish hangouts. The trout along this side are apt to be concentrated closer to the bank, thus offering anglers a more desirable-looking target area to cast to. Grass-bordered banks are another good possibility. Fish can be used to hoppers, crickets, beetles, ants, and

TYPICAL FISH LOCATIONS

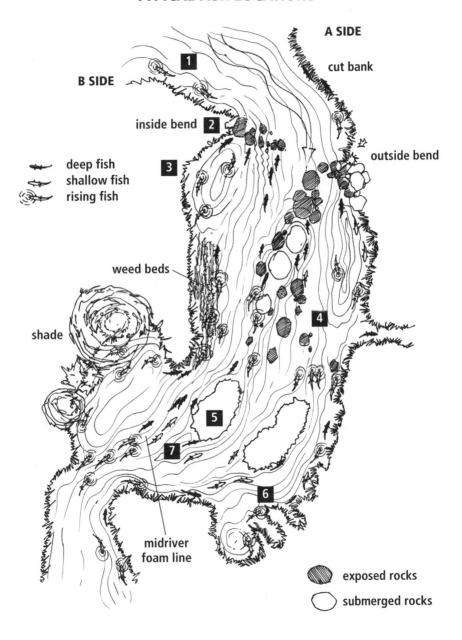

A SIDE

cut bank

B SIDE

1

inside bend 2

outside bend

deep fish
shallow fish
rising fish

3

weed beds

shade

4

5

7

6

midriver
foam line

exposed rocks

submerged rocks

other land-based insects as part of their diet. Such fish can be easier to fool with a broader array of patterns.

Both anglers will want to cast to the most likely-looking spots all through the day. The bow angler will hit such hot spots first. The stern angler will hit them immediately afterward. Other water might be ignored. Unless the bow fisherman is a bad caster and really not covering these spots well the first time, the stern rod would be better off covering a different drift lane than the first rod did. And unless one hot fly pattern has already proven to be the best, floating anglers might do better trying varying fly types.

For instance, the bow angler could fish a dry fly a few feet out from the bank, targeting subtle eddy lines and drop-offs, while the stern angler drops a streamer, nymph, or contrasting dry fly closer in. In this way, you cover two feeding lanes rather than one and experiment with a variety of flies until you find the ones that work the best. These hot patterns are likely to change with time and in different water types. In this way, too, the bow angler doesn't hit the close-in water at all, thus leaving the stern angler some unfished, unspooked trout.

The center of the river undoubtedly holds some fish, but it's such a flat, monotonous, and possibly deep glide of water that few will choose to fish it. Skilled indicator nymphers will get their share here. A deep-swimming, well-sunk streamer on a full sinking line would be a possibility, but it's a possibility most will ignore. During a profuse hatch, trout could be rising here and there out in the middle, especially if a big foam line wanders downstream. In this case, the fish are giving themselves away and make good targets. On the whole, though, most floaters will choose one side or the other in such a stretch.

Along the B side of the river at position 1 is a slower-paced, shallow sheet of water that looks uniform, boring, and unproductive. However, there can be quite a few trout (and whitefish) scattered along here. Some nice fish will hold surprisingly

Big trout often rise in slow, shallow water, where it's easy for them to feed without fighting the current. This nice brown took a Two-lone PMD on the Missouri, where I spend most of my guide days.

close to the shore in just inches of water because few anglers bother them and chase them out. (The trout's entire feeding universe is compressed in shallow water. They can rise or nymph from the same position.) Because trout here are scattered and sparse, most floaters choose the A side. But when a good hatch is on, a surprising number of trout can materialize along this slower side, giving excellent match-the-hatch fishing. In that case, it can be better to pull over and wade-fish to those steady risers. The uniform flows make presentations easy, but the clear water allows fish to look over your fly, and they can be picky and spooky.

It's always a good idea to stop and concentrate on a good hatch. You never know when the wind might come up in the West—these could be the last rising fish you see for the day! On the other hand, a perfect day might show you so many rising fish and therefore slow your progress down so much that you'll have to navigate your way off the river in the dark if you don't pay attention to your time and mileage schedule.

If no hatch is on along the B side, it's most effectively fished by using long drifts of a dry fly (with each angler's fly covering different feed lanes), by dry fly and nymph combinations, or by streamer fishing. Streamers should be dropped up close to the bank and fished all the way back to the boat, for trout can be widely scattered. This covers a lot of water, and you can gaze around at the scenery, something that many forget to do!

As we proceed downriver from position 1 to position 2, we enter what's known as the tail of the pool, or the tailout. The streambed often widens here temporarily and becomes shallow. Trout are fond of rising here during good hatches due to the gradually upsloping bottom and slowing currents. They can be spread all the way across the river. When not rising, they'll seem nonexistent or widely scattered. A standing bow angler (front of boat) wearing polarized glasses will see these scattered fish. They'll often be fleeing, as they see him, too. During a profuse hatch, this can be a prime area to anchor and wade. You could drop one fisherman off on one side of the river, row across, anchor on the other side, and fish there, too. Anglers could then work their way up both sides or to wherever fish are sighted. Many tailouts allow an easy row across the river without sweeping the boat downstream. Others have swifter centers and take more power to cross.

Position 2

As we approach position 2, the river makes a sharp curve, eroding one side and often leaving a gravel beach on the other. This is a classic pool-riffle-pool sequence on a big-river scale. It can be a real hot spot with fish concentrated behind the drop-off on the inside bend (the B side). You can float-fish it, making a point of not rowing over the best trout water, and then pull over below and walk back up to wade-fish.

There can be a variety of fish-holding spots here. Along bank A are usually some swift-water pockets that hold fish. From a boat, these are often one-shot deals, because the current can be whisking you along at a pretty good rate, even if you are back-rowing like mad. It's good attractor-dry, nymph, and streamer water, and big fish might be found. You can float-fish this outside bend, then cross over, anchor, and wade-fish the riffle drop-off on the inside bend. You could also drop one angler off along that steeper outside bend to fish his way back up, covering those enticing pockets thoroughly.

Downstream in the center is a drop-off, sometimes rock- and boulder-studded, that is capable of housing many trout. This is a deep-nymphing prospect. If you can get your nymphs (or streamers) to the bottom and fish it systematically while wade-fishing, you may be in for a treat. You could float-fish it, too, with heavy nymphs, weighted leaders, and strike indica- tors. If you catch a fish there, you can row back upstream along the slower B side bank, and float-fish it again. This is known as a row-around, and it can be repeated as long as it works. It's better to pull over and wade-fish the center, time allowing. In these days of heavier fishing pressure, though, explore and per- fect all alternatives, including midriver nymphing from the boat.

Closer to the B bank, the drop-off becomes shallow. It's eas- ier to cover and can hold concentrations of trout, especially on big tailwater rivers. A dry fly and nymph combination is a good starting setup. During a hatch, you might find many rising fish, though they can be tougher to spot in the choppy waves. Some will move surprisingly close to the bank in ultrashallow water, including the largest rising fish. Indicator nymphing is always a good bet here, and streamers work well, too.

When a boat floats by such drop-offs, expectations are high. The rower should slow down as much as possible as the

Inside bends on big tailwater rivers show broad riffles with numerous trout. These are great locations to stop and wade-fish. You'll often find rising trout, and nymphing can be excellent.

anglers cover different feed lanes. You should target any distinct eddy lines. Doubles are possible in this type of water. It's an area to concentrate on between hatches if the mood to wade-fish strikes you, and a great place to find rising fish as well when the hatches come.

Position 3

Just behind the actual drop-off on the B side is a distinct eddy known to some as the eye of the pool. In some cases, the current just moderates, with no back-swirling eddy being formed. Either way, it's a favorite spot for trout to hold in. Food is abundant, and they can fin easily in the slower water. The sanctuary of midriver is but a few wiggles away. Trout can be scattered across this eddy zone, from the deep bank out to what's often a distinct but broadening eddy line. On smaller water, there might just be one or two fish. It can be roughly covered from the boat, but the boat's motion and the eddying currents make it hard to get a long drift of the fly. The line can start dragging before some trout will choose to take. (Gung-ho wilderness trout can be eager enough to jump on it when it first lands.) Stopping to wade-fish the eye is best, after first scouting it for the noses of rising fish.

Out across midstream near position 3 is the belly of the pool. It's usually deep, rock-studded, and fish-holding. On gravel-bottom rivers, there are drop-offs and depressions that also will contain trout. It's deep nymph and streamer territory, except on small, shallow rivers where fish might take surface flies without having to come up through too much water. There can be plenty of fish spread over a large area, including schools of whitefish and many trout. Time allowing, this, too, could be wade-fished most effectively. Otherwise, a couple of row-arounds could be in order.

Along the deeper A side of position 3 is often a steeper eroded bank. It can be rock-studded and have some high-water log debris left there. Bank pockets and riffle lines are numerous. It's the kind of float-fishing water that has great eye appeal and fish, too, though there are usually more overall trout back on the B side in positions 2 to 3. Nonetheless, it's a fish producer.

Trout will rise here during a hatch and take attractor patterns if the mood hits. It's excellent nymph water almost any-time. Trout are used to grabbing naturals that wash out of the fast water upstream. A dry fly with a nymph dropper is a good choice, too, as are indicator nymphs and streamers. Many feeding trout prefer to sit upstream of rocks along these types of banks and in the river's center, rather than behind them. This is something to remember when fishing broken pocketwater.

The boatman should do his best to slow the boat down to a near standstill while the anglers cover different feed lanes and pockets, as many as possible. It's not usually a good place to anchor a boat. The swift current can actually pull the stern end of the boat underwater when it is anchored in too heavy a flow. The boat can also swing wildly from side to side on the anchor rope and possibly flip. In other cases, the anchor won't hold and will be dragged downstream. Sometimes the anchor will snag among rocks and prove to be irretrievable. It will have to be cut loose. I always consider bottom structure and current speed before dropping my anchor.

A good way to fish the pocketwater along the fast-water bank is to pull the boat over near the tailout after float-fishing it and let one angler get out of the boat and systematically fish his way back up. Few people take advantage of this productive tactic. (Know your state's trespass laws, though.)

Position 4

As the river slows and widens, it fans out into the tail of the pool, much as in position 1. In this case, its character differs, eventually splitting into an island system.

On spring-rich and tailwater rivers, the B side here will grow profuse weed beds and support many trout. During a hatch, many steady-rising fish will give their positions away on the expansive flats. This is great water to wade and hunt for big noses and pulsing wakes during a hatch.

Midriver could be shallow enough to still show rising trout. It could also just deepen into a zone of little interest. Some big trout can hold upstream of islands and fall victim to indicator nymphs or wide-swept streamers fished deep.

The A bank could continue to have rock pockets, though with a mellower flow. It, too, could widen into tailout flats. Either way, it's likely to hold fish and be a fun area to cover. It's a good place to be during a hatch and also fishes well blind

Tailouts are favorite places for trout to rise —on small rivers, at the lower end of a pool, and on big tailwaters, in hundreds of yards of shallowing flats.

because there's often enough definition (for instance, ripple lines, pockets) to make targeting imagined fish practical.

This is easy water to row. Fish that are seen can be picked off from the boat. Note that fish see standing anglers in a boat from a greater distance than seated ones. If trout are spooky, sit and cast. The rower should be able to hold the boat in place in the current or anchor within ideal casting range of specific targets. Let your anchor down slowly, though. It can scare fish when it thuds on the bottom and scrapes across the gravel before holding. The streambed of a tailout is generally formed of finer gravel and cobblestones that settle out of the current after tumbling through the faster water drop-off upstream in high water. It's normally a good anchoring and wading area that will have rising trout.

I do a lot of sight-fishing anchored. Ease the anchor down well upstream of the fish, endeavoring to end up at a 45-degree angle upstream of the target, in reasonable casting range. If the trout seem spooky, sit to cast, as trout can see standing anglers at a greater distance. Success was achieved here with pinpoint casting and a good reach cast during a Trico spinnerfall.

Position 5

Island systems are frequently formed from erosion as rivers cut corners and carve new channels. The usual scenario sees islands loom into view at the tailout of one run and form part of the drop-off that heads the next one. Series of gravel bars, some connecting island to island, can be found. Their riffles, eddy lines, streambed depressions, and drop-offs all hold the promise of trout. The river becomes shallow as it approaches the head of the island (the upstream end). Trout like to hold in these tailouts and feed during a hatch.

Gravel bars can lead from bank to island and island to island. Sometimes you can wade across them, though on big rivers perhaps not. In either case, there are likely to be gravel bar drop-offs and depressions that can be good places to nymph blind or to spot rising fish during a hatch.

Next come the ripple lines that peel off the heads of islands and the slower fish-holding water just downstream of them. These can be much like the situation back at position 2, side B, but on a smaller, gentler scale. They can be excellent dry-fly riffles. Nymphs, two-fly rigs, and streamers all might work. Trout may be stacked in here.

At the ends of islands, converging currents, drop-offs, and eddies can be great indicator-nymphing locations between hatches, with trout ganged up in this ideal holding water. During a hatch, some rising fish will push forward closer to the drop-off. Others might fall back or follow slow-coursing foam lanes, rising where food concentrates most.

It's always a good idea to stop and look for rising trout before blindly wading in to cast. Check the shallow water nearest the island banks first, and scan out from there. During a good hatch, you can pinpoint all the possible targets and then proceed to fish for them in an order least likely to scare subsequent risers off. You might land several good trout from the same casting position. Islands are always favorite places to stop and wade-fish.

Thinking about how to maximize your opportunities can lead to more fish caught. For instance, if you wade-fish the ripple line peeling off the head of a small island first, the silt you kick up could put down the trout that were rising in the drop-off at the tail. It would be better to look over the whole situation, start fishing the tail, and then work your way back up to the head. You'll even want to watch where you pull in your boat to land, making sure you don't row over rising fish or the most likely trout-holding water.

On larger rivers, trout show a fondness for smaller side channels. They often concentrate there, sometimes in surprising numbers. It seems as if they prefer the confinement of a small channel over the universe of wide-open water. If no rising fish are found, get nymphs down near the bottom, or sweep a

This boat is slowing to fish the converging currents at the bottom end of an island. When steadily rising trout are found here, anchor to work them thoroughly. Depending on the water depth and speed, you may have to anchor well in advance to get the boat to stop where you want it.

streamer. You can often fish a streamer first and pull out the most aggressive fish, wait a couple minutes, and then go back through with an indicator nymph and pick off more. A couple of switches in nymph patterns might yield additional fish. On freestone rivers, medium to large nymphs can produce best (but not always). On tailwaters and spring-fed rivers, small nymphs are likely to be better choices. Fishing two varying nymphs at a time is a good idea, too. Experiment with different sizes, colors, and patterns.

Position 6

Position 6 finds us at a deeply eroded bank littered with flood debris and overhanging logs. Little foam lanes trickle across the dark slow pool, leading down from the ripple drop-off back up the side channel. Such spots are common enough and most always house some trout. If the hillside behind is steep and light reflection is blocked, trout here can often be spotted cruising just beneath the surface, as trout are wont to do. Others will stay under the cover of the bank, showing themselves but occasionally. Still others might stay deep, feeding on what the side channel brings in. I know of many locations like this.

Some trout here can be spotted, stalked, and caught from a rowed or anchored boat. Rowing the boat to a standstill should be no problem in water like this. It's always fun and educational to stalk visible trout; there's something to learn about trout behavior in every encounter. If no fish are in evidence, a Woolly Bugger here is a good choice. You could also systematically cover the water with a nymph or large dry like a hopper or Stimulator. A big twitched dry can draw some fish to the surface from afar.

Position 7

Below the island system, side channels reconverge and the gravel bar drop-offs (some of which can be extensive) can hold trout. During a hatch, you might find risers concentrated in subtle eddies behind minichannels that pour over such bars. Fish can also stack up in the upper part of the regrouped channel. The bottom configuration gives them shelter from the current while dumping in plenty of food. This is another spot that's best fished by pulling over and nymphing systematically. Some fish may be rising during hatches, but more might be caught deep.

When floating, you can hold the boat just behind riffle drop-offs with surprising ease. As the water drops over a gravel bar into a trough, it creates a minihole that's not visible yet helps to hold the boat in place. A rower can move back and forth across such drop-offs, letting anglers cover the water before rowing over it. You can row across a river behind a gravel bar in this fashion with little effort. You could anchor, too, and jump out to wade-fish if it's shallow enough, though some less agile anglers might have a hard time getting back up into the boat. Watch for loose gravel at the drop-off edge, or you could slide and sink into much deeper water and be carried off downstream.

Position 8

Here we see a slow, deep channel and rather featureless water accented with a wandering midriver foam line. Watch these closely during and after a hatch or spinnerfall. Trout can gather and cruise there, rising to the food that concentrates in such foam. The current can be slow enough that trout can hold there all day. Sometimes you just see rings of rising fish. Other times, in more ideal viewing conditions, you can see the fish finning just below the surface and looking to it for a meal.

Position 9

The point on side B at position 9 is similar to that back at positions 2 and 3, but the current is slower and the surface smoother. Some bits of foam and weed might be found circulating in the eddy here, and it's a good place to find a few rising fish during and especially after a hatch. Some might push up into and fan out along the edge of the eddy line. Others cruise the big quiet eddy or hold near the bank edge.

This bank is deep and bordered by trees, which provide shade that gives fish cover from the sun and predatory birds (while also giving these same birds a place to perch!), plus an added source of food in the form of terrestrial insects. In very hot weather, the shade might even indicate the few places you'll find actively feeding fish. I like to row a boat to a standstill in such spots and look hard for cruising trout. Some might ease in and out of view beneath the foliage and require exacting casts. Sometimes, sitting and watching for a while can be more productive than immediately slapping a fly down. On the other

Big eddies circulate insects during and after hatches. Trout can continue rising here when those in the mainstream have ceased. Look giant eddies over carefully for the noses of big trout.

hand, I recall casting damselfly dry flies down in spots like this and seeing trout come zooming over to pounce on them. Those slow, shady spots are always worth an extra minute or two of inspection time, regardless of the outcome. A slow-swimming Woolly Bugger, twitched dry, or a twist-retrieved nymph might pull out a fish.

Although it would be impossible to mention every river and trout-holding configuration, this short trip certainly covers many of them. A good hatch makes it easier to explore a new reach of river, for the fish then give their positions away. Even between hatches, some fish will rise. Others can be seen under the water by those who constantly look for them, especially a standing angler in the bow. Polarized sunglasses and a backdrop that blocks glare from the sky help immensely. And of course, there are big trout that rarely rise and can't be seen. Successful float fishers will be imagining where the best trout water should be while keeping their eyes peeled for surface and subsurface trout throughout the day.

ROWING A CASTING PLATFORM

An oarsman can help anglers in several ways. He's an integral part of the fishing and not a detached onlooker. It's a teamwork effort that works best if all in the party are on top of their game. The boat is nothing more than a rowed platform from which to cast. Whether it's near the bank, upstream, outside, or downstream of its quarry, its position and motion should be deliberately chosen to produce the desired results.

The rower's first priority (besides safety) is to slow the boat down by steadily back rowing to give anglers time to assess the water (on both sides and in the center of the river), to look for risers and subsurface trout, and to cover the river as thoroughly as possible. Equally important is keeping the craft a steady distance from the bank or target water as much as possible so that fly casters can work with a uniform length of line. You shouldn't

CASTING FARTHER DOWNSTREAM

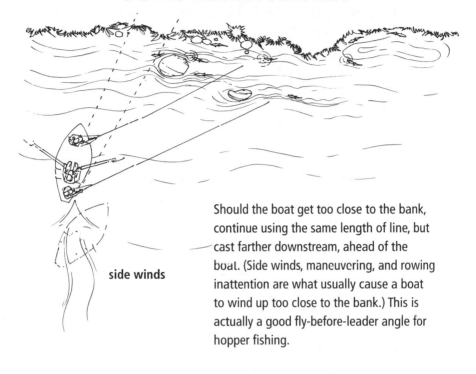

side winds

Should the boat get too close to the bank, continue using the same length of line, but cast farther downstream, ahead of the boat. (Side winds, maneuvering, and rowing inattention are what usually cause a boat to wind up too close to the bank.) This is actually a good fly-before-leader angle for hopper fishing.

be so close as to scare fish off or so far as to make casting time-consuming, difficult, or impossible. Thirty-five to fifty feet away would be a good generic working distance. On shallow, ripply, and rough-surfaced rivers, you can get a little closer to the fish without them seeing you. On deeper, slow, slick-surfaced rivers, you'll need to stay a little farther away and perhaps sit while casting so the fish don't see you.

There will be times, of course, when the rower can't keep a specific distance from a bank and will have to get closer to it. This is usually either due to a narrow channel or because of executing a hazard maneuver. Sometimes the current or wind will inadvertently push you closer into a bank than you meant to go (as will inattention to your duties). What anglers can do in these cases, besides the obvious choice of shortening their lines, is to cast farther downstream from the boat using the same length of line. The boat can be pushed right up against the bank, and they can still continue to fish effectively. They'll have to be on guard to avoid tangling lines, but a more downstream, rather than across-stream, presentation will certainly fool a high percentage of fish while allowing casters to go on using the same length of line.

If the rower has to pull farther away from the target water to miss a hazard, the casters can either lengthen line or fish around the hazard. You don't want to lengthen your fly line to an extreme degree, because it then becomes more and more likely that you might hook someone in the boat on a bad cast. You could also just let your fly drag out from the bank and appreciate the panoramic scenery for a moment. It's surprising how many fish are caught when a fly is allowed to skitter across deeper water.

As the boatman back-rows his way downstream, his eyes and mind constantly scan the river, summing up the most likely trout water. He might ferry back and forth across-stream numerous times, choosing trout zones and putting anglers within casting range of the most likely ones. He'll maneuver more to gain the best fishing positions than to avoid hazards. Back-rowing intensity will vary, too: an easy pace for mediocre stretches, a vigorous yet quiet pace for extra-productive-looking spots (you don't want to scare fish with splashy oar strokes or boat noise). You might row to a standstill, anchor, or disembark to wade-fish a prime location, or you might go a little more with the flow to deep-nymph a midriver weed bed. (Vigorous back rowing won't allow a nymph to sink deeply and get a long drift.) Each water type can call for a slightly different approach, both in boat speed and position.

The position of a boat in relation to a fish or a hot spot can be important to success. There are any number of positions you

There is a perfect casting distance and angle to optimize success in most cases. Waiting for that perfect moment ups your odds. Here, a brown was taken in a tricky current line along the rock.

could be in that are 40 feet from your target—upstream, directly across, downstream, to the inside, or to the outside. But only one of them might allow the perfect drift of your fly over the fish without undue drag—just being within casting range isn't always enough.

For this reason, the oarsman must also be considering things from the fly caster's point of view, something that many novice rowers initially fail to comprehend. When I guide, I'm thinking largely of the fly line and its optimal angle and placement in relation to a trout. I know there's a certain distance that can be managed by each caster, and one best angle of approach. Remember that the boat is usually out toward midriver in swifter water, whereas the fish is in closer to the bank in slower currents. There can be eddies and current variances in between, too. I often tell my guests that I'm going to ease slowly into the perfect position and then tell them when to cast. Human nature leads some to cast a little early, when the fish really isn't in perfect range yet. It's eagerness that steers them. The fly usually starts dragging just as it comes up to the trout's position. If they had waited until I floated 5 feet closer, the perfect drift could have been achieved. This kind of subtlety is very important when casting to larger, spookier rising fish.

Casting from a boat is in some ways the opposite of wade-fishing a stream. The latter sees most casts made upstream and across-stream. Anglers often wade in slower water near the bank and cast up into swift water. Float fishers are generally doing things the other way around: They're in swift water casting to slow water. What works best from the boat is to cast somewhat downstream at close to a 45-degree angle (see illustration). The line must land with some slack built into it, though. It then straightens as it approaches its target. I might stop back rowing for a few seconds or even row forward just a bit to help extend the drift of a dry fly I think is going to pass perfectly over a trout's position. (Vigorous back rowing naturally tends to straighten the leader and causes drag at a faster rate.) After the fly passes beyond the trout's position, I might then back-row like mad, possibly returning upstream a bit to regain the ideal casting angle.

Once you get even with or just downstream of a trout or a pocket, that swifter current near the boat makes it harder and harder to get a long drag-free drift. There are ways to do it, but it's easier and better to get a longer drift from a slightly up-stream angle.

Let's briefly consider the merits, subtleties, and difficulties of casting to a fish from different boat positions (see the illustration). These could be while the boat is being rowed or anchored.

Position 1

Once in a while, a rising fish will be spotted in such a position that the only probable angle for a good drift will be from directly upstream. I find this most along steeper rocky banks where little channels between boulders and swirling eddies make presentations from other angles difficult at best. The fish is spotted, the situation is assessed, and the boat is pulled in parallel to the bank at a workable casting distance.

You could drop the anchor here, but be careful about stirring up bottom silt, which could put the fish down. I often choose to row using the crawl stroke. The sweeping oar is nearest the bank. Sometimes you can just lay the bankside oar across some rocks and half-wedge it there while making easy backstrokes with the midriver oar.

The caster needs to use an extreme slack-line cast and perhaps feed additional line out to get the fly over the trout. If it doesn't take on the first couple of drifts, the fish could easily spook, because you now have to retrieve leader and fly back upstream by the trout before making another cast. A little extra time and stealth between casts so as not to alert the fish can win the day. An extra-long light tippet helps, too. I have guests who catch plenty of trout this way. Obviously, only one angler can fish in this situation.

Position 2

The boat in position 2 is at the best overall angle for most float-fishing presentations. A down-and-across presentation using a slack-line reach cast allows long drag-free drifts, even across

BOAT POSITION AND CASTING

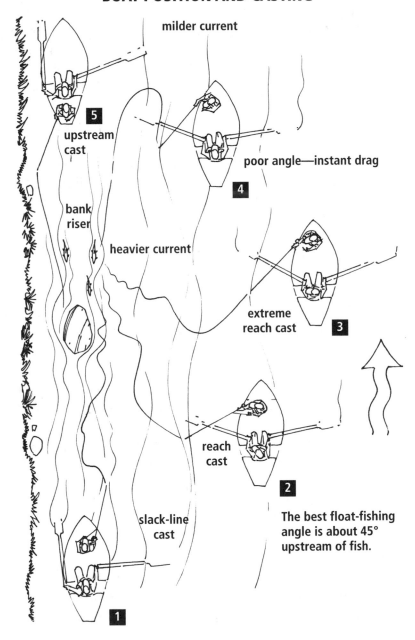

milder current

5

upstream cast

bank riser

heavier current

poor angle—instant drag

4

extreme reach cast

3

reach cast

2

slack-line cast

1

The best float-fishing angle is about 45° upstream of fish.

eddy lines. It also shows trout the fly before the leader, which helps fool pickier fish. It's an easy cast to do—every float fisher needs to master it (see the illustration). The reach cast is the single most important cast when fishing from drift boats.

From position 2 to position 3 will be your best bet generally. The boatman may be able to row the boat to a standstill here. I'll often anchor at position 2 to work a trout or school of rising fish more thoroughly. You have to slow your boat down and plan to drop anchor before you get to the actual position, because the boat will end up downstream of the anchor itself and may drag it a bit before it takes hold. Trout can spook when an anchor hits the bottom and drags. They'll usually resume rising in a minute or two, though, so wait them out. The denser the hatch, the sooner they'll resume rising. You can wait them out if you spook them with casts, too. Sometimes it's best to pause a while between presentations to keep from frightening the fish. Sitting while casting can be preferred.

Position 3
When you reach the point where you're even with your fish, long dead-drift presentations start becoming more difficult to achieve. The act of casting directly across the main current and eddy lines now has a more immediate effect on your fly line. Drag sets in quicker than it did from the slightly upstream position.

Here again, a slack-line reach cast is best. It can be a little more extreme, with the rod reached upstream as far as you can easily manage. This allows you to show your fly to the fish before the leader and achieves the longest possible drag-free presentations. If you were to cast a straight line to the fish, as many anglers habitually do, drag would set in almost immediately. A few overenthusiastic trout will take a dragging fly, but many more will engulf a well-presented fly on a reach cast. An immediate mend might be necessary, too.

Position 4

Once you are downstream of the fish, it becomes difficult to get much of a drag-free drift. The main current quickly grabs your fly line no matter how it's cast and begins dragging it away. A skilled caster might use a tuck cast with some extra slack built in and buy a little time, but this is decidedly a tough angle for dry-fly work from a drift boat unless it is in a giant eddy, uniformly flowing, or a very slow stretch or river. When you're fishing streamers, however, many trout seem to like the down-and-across angle in which the wet fly swims. Perhaps it better imitates a baitfish in trouble. In any case, many fish are caught with Woolly Buggers and similar streamers fished from various angles to the banks.

Anglers usually find themselves fishing from position 4 only when the rower can't keep them in position 2 or 3 due to current speed. It might be worth trying that last shot back upstream to a rising fish or hot spot. When just fishing the water with no rising fish in sight, anglers will want to maintain a slightly down-and-across angle of their fly lines for the longest drag-free drifts. Don't look back, look ahead!

Position 5

Should that trout still be rising after the boat has drifted by, it's a good idea to pull over along the bank and try from below. You can anchor, row to a standstill, or let an angler out on the bank. This will be a classic up-and-over casting approach, familiar to every wade and bank fisher. Some guides will jump out and walk the boat upstream into casting range, either bow or stern first, depending on which angler's turn it is to have a go at the fish. Taking turns casting in one-fish situations is the name of the game. This avoids fly-line tangles and is less likely to spook fish. If you see a number of trout rising in a row tight to a productive bank, you may opt to land below them all, walk the bank back upstream, and work one fish at a time. I generally

ANCHOR HOPPING

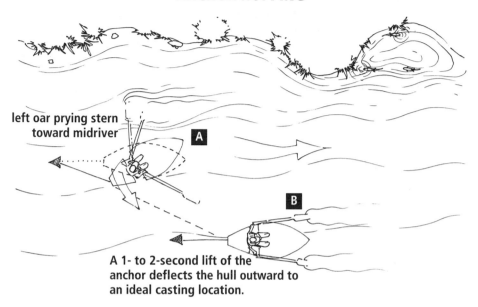

left oar prying stern toward midriver

A

B

A 1- to 2-second lift of the anchor deflects the hull outward to an ideal casting location.

Anchor hopping fine-tunes the boat's position for an optimal casting angle (and optimal distance).

A. Upon seeing rising fish ahead, the rower quietly anchors in advance, knowing the anchor may drag a ways before holding. Then he moves slightly to a more ideal spot. While anchored on a short rope, he pulls hard several times on the left oar, angling his stern toward midriver. A one- or two-second lift of the anchor deflects the current off the hull, where it anchors at **B**.

prefer to try them first from the boat, using the down and across cast from position 2. Some trout seem less wary when approached from this direction. If anglers can't make good, controlled reach casts, then fishing from below is a good backup option. Watch for bushes on your backcast.

Every river encounter is a little different, but all need to be assessed in order to find and capitalize on the best angle of presentation for the angler. It's the rower's job to put and keep the boat in that position as long as necessary or possible. (The anchor can be a boatman's best friend.) A quick conference between rower and casters might be in order to decide what that position is, but no time should be wasted in planning the course of action. When doing a straightforward "float by," anglers must recognize that there is a premium angle and moment to drop that fly in a trout's feed lane. Skilled casters will be able to stretch the limits of that angle to a greater degree.

As you row into position, avoid kicking up waves with the boat and oars. This can put fish down in calmer waters. Some anglers use too much body motion when casting and rock the boat from side to side, putting out waves that can scare flat-water trout. Also avoid dropping things in the boat or making loud, clunking sounds, which transmit from boat hull to water.

One can get only so close to a trout before it sees the boat and flees. The flatter and deeper the water, the easier trout can spot you. Beginning fly fishers may have a difficult time casting far enough with the proper accuracy and control to fool rising fish on some calm rivers. They would do better on swifter, choppier rivers, where the trout's vision is obscured by waves, which means you can approach them more closely. Such trout tend to be "grabbier," too.

The rower can also help out once a trout takes a fly. Trout holding near a bank often race for midstream when hooked, which is right at the boat. Trout will run toward the boat, by it, or even under it, and then continue on toward midriver. This can make it difficult for an angler to reel up line fast enough to keep the fish under tension. I'll often start back-rowing away from the bank when a fish takes, anticipating this likely scenario. This can help an angler keep a tight line on his trout as it runs for midstream. If the fish just wallows near the bank or runs in some different direction, I'll adjust my rowing to the situation. You'll need to follow some fish downstream or lead them away from tangling cover. The boat can play a strategic role in landing a fine specimen. The rower or other angler can also do the netting, which can help increase the odds of success. Some anglers prefer fighting their trout from the bank, in which case the rower can drop them at the bank, making sure the boat is out of the angler's way.

All these aspects of float fishing will come into play at some time in future journeys. Anticipating the possibilities improves your fishing day.

5

Fly-Fishing Strategies

Fly fishing from a boat requires special know-how. Because the casters and rower are in close proximity, safe casting becomes a major concern. So does avoiding tangles. A number of specialized casts come into play, while refined mending tactics add trout to the tally. Making these strategies habitual will polish your game.

Because anglers in a boat often cast simultaneously, they need to keep their flies on parallel flight paths. Whenever they deviate from this general rule, tangles on the backcast or forward cast are bound to happen. Taking turns casting is best. It's easier for the angler in the back of the boat to watch the bow angler and cast when he's finished. A little verbal communication about your casting intentions helps, too, especially if you're about to cast out of parallel. For instance, when you are making a last upstream cast to a rising fish the boat has drifted by, tell the other angler when you're about to cast out of sync, so he can hold off from casting and watch your glory shot. Parallel casts at a slight downstream angle (up to 45 degrees) are generally the name of the game.

Distance casting, casting in high winds, and the fishing of extra-heavy nymphs and streamers call for added attention, for

TWO ANGLERS CASTING FROM A BOAT

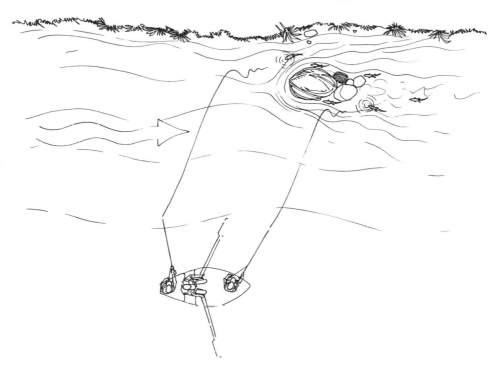

Fly fishing from a boat calls for new mindsets. Anglers cast parallel with each other at a forward angle (up to 45 degrees) using reach casts. Taking turns casting results in fewer tangles. Verbal communication helps. Keep backcasts high and tight to avoid hooking others. The bow angler (in the front) can target outer feed lanes, while the stern angler hits those closer to the bank. Divide and conquer. Sitting anglers are less visible to fish than standing ones. Wear clothes that camouflage you with the sky, and avoid rocking the boat, which makes waves.

the chances of hooking a boatmate are higher in these conditions. Make sure there is no slack line on the water when you begin your backcast. Slack line on the water during a line pickup is the most common cause of both tangles and getting hooked. Strip your fly line in and start your backcast on a tight

When two anglers fish from drift boats, they should take turns casting to avoid midair tangles. Generally, they'll be casting parallel with each other, at a downstream 45-degree angle.

line with your rod tip held low near the water. Make your backcasts extra high to clear the boat's crew. Watch some of your backcasts to make sure their flight paths stay high. A sudden scream usually indicates a low backcast and the subsequent low and dangerous forward cast!

The stern angler has to be aware of the rower's oar strokes. When the boatman reaches back with the oars to begin his next stroke, they often cross the path of the stern angler's drifting fly line. The stern angler needs to lift his fly rod a bit to allow the oar to pass under his fly line; otherwise, frequent tangles between line and oar will ensue. He must do this consistently to keep from ruining the rower's cadence, positioning, and peace of mind! The rower should not be interrupted by the stern angler's fly line, especially in critical maneuvering moments.

When anglers have mastered safe and controlled casting, all parties can focus on covering and exploring the water with a fly. (It's amazing how many hours of a fishing day can be spent untangling lines when the casters aren't in sync.) Visible rising fish aside, anglers should cover eligible-looking water as systematically as possible. The rower does his part by assessing the water and his positioning and by slowing the craft so that anglers can pick up their fly at the end of its drift, make a false cast or two, and drop the fly back out where the last drift ended.

Anglers should run their flies down different feed lanes to cover the water best. The first rod, in the front of the boat, can run his a little way out from the bank. The stern rod can fish closer in. In this way, a broader zone of the river is covered, and both casters have an equal chance of success. Some water types such as deep undercut banks present single, defined targets and both anglers will want to run their flies over the same lanes and pockets. Other times, though, eddies, pockets, and ripple lines against, near, and peeling out from the bank present the two anglers with a broader zone of potential fish water that's best covered by fishing different lanes.

Fishing two-fly rigs allows you to cover even more water. Flies can be spaced 1 to 3 feet apart, offering fish both a dry and a nymph, while widening the zone covered by both anglers a little farther. Having the stern rod sweep a streamer (or two) covers even more trouty terrain. Should one fly pattern prove to be the best producer, you could fish it alone or tie two on.

SPECIAL CASTING TECHNIQUES

A few casting adaptations make fishing from a boat more productive. The reach cast is most important. Every float fisher should master this simple technique, because one can achieve up to three times the length of a dead-drifted fly by using it. Whether you are fishing dry flies, nymphs, or even streamers, this technique should improve your catch rate.

The Reach Cast
The way to get the longest drag-free drift of your fly while floating is to cast at a downstream angle using the reach cast. This
simple ploy is indispensable in many fishing situations.

Begin by making a straight overhead cast (not a sidearm
one) at about a 45-degree downstream angle. Make your cast a
little higher than usual, with a bit of extra power. As your line
begins to turn over above its intended landing site, slowly and
smoothly reach your rod upstream as far as you comfortably
can before your line or fly hits the water. Line should still be
shooting through the rod's eyes as you reach. After reaching
your arm and rod upstream, and when the fly line and leader
fully extend, drop your rod tip, line, and fly gently to the water.
The fly should now go over the fish before the leader does.
(When a fish takes, you have to pause half a second before setting the hook, allowing the trout to head back under; otherwise, you might pull the fly right out of the mouth of larger
slow-rising trout.) As your line and fly float downstream, follow
their progress with your rod tip. The cast lands with you reaching upstream, and you follow the fly until you're reaching
downstream. This 15-plus feet of rod tip and arm movement
allows very long drag-free drifts of a fly.

To add more slack, which is always a good idea at the beginning of a dry fly or nymph drift, make a slightly more powerful
forward cast. Upon completely unfurling, the line will spring
back a bit, creating some slack. This happens while you are
reaching upstream. In some cases, you'll want to cast beyond
your targeted feed lane, since the reach and bounce-back effect
will draw your fly back toward you somewhat.

For even more slack, wiggle the rod tip up and down while
you reach. At the same time, release some extra line through
the rod guides. Now you should have plenty of slack built into
the drift of line and fly for extra-long drag-free drifts. These can
be necessary for some rising-fish situations, as well as when

THE REACH CAST

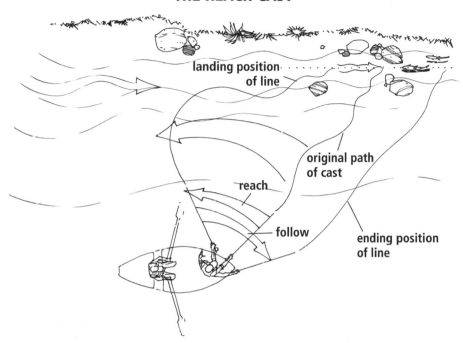

landing position
of line

original path
of cast

reach

follow

ending position
of line

The reach cast lengthens drag-free drifts of a dry fly or nymph severalfold. It allows the streamers to sink deeper as well. It should become float-fishing habit, used on almost every cast.

covering the water. They help immensely in thwarting drag when casting into bank eddies and across swirling eddy lines. When you are deep nymphing, long drifts allow the fly to sink to the proper level, for only then is it beginning to do its job. It's often advantageous to cast streamers on a slack line, too, letting them sink a while along a bank before retrieving. This helps get them deep. When trout are slow to move to a fly, dead-drifted deep streamers can work better than stripped ones.

Even good slack-line reach casts may need to be mended in the traditional fashion. The swifter water near the boat will

Stack mends and long-distance drifts come in handy for midriver nymphing, hopper fishing, and extended presentations to sighted fish.

want to belly your line downstream. Throwing a little upstream mend just after your fly lands is a good habit to develop. Roll line both upstream and toward the bank you're fishing while releasing more line through your rod's guides. This keeps from putting tension on the line and leader that's already on the water, which would pull out the slack you created and drag your fly. Mends should always be made as anticipatory maneuvers, not as last-ditch efforts.

Stack Mends
The ultimate long drift combines an extreme reach cast with stack mends. Stack mends are made by flipping several loose lengths of fly line toward the fly and its intended path. Drop your rod tip low and use quick little up-and-out flicks of the tip to propel extra line in the direction of your fly. I believe up-and-down wiggles are better than side-to-side ones. They aren't usually rolled upstream, as most mends are. The end result is a lot of slack line on the water that slowly straightens out as boat and fly line float downstream. I use this method most when indicator nymphing and when fishing two-fly rigs, hoppers, and attractor dry flies. Long drifts cover a lot of water when you are fishing blind. Sometimes stack mends are needed to sneak a fly over a rising fish, too, especially from directly upstream through the 45-degree standard angle.

Should a trout take your fly just after you stack mend a lot of slack on the water, a comic scene can follow. You'll strip line in like mad while leaning backward until you almost fall over. It can be difficult to tighten up and set the hook. The rower can help tighten that line a little by quickly rowing away from the fish. I'll also set the hook by mending line in such a situation. A big power mend or two that throws your line toward midriver can get rid of all the slack and set the hook at the same time. If you mend quickly and vigorously enough, the trout will be

STACK MENDS AND POWER MEND

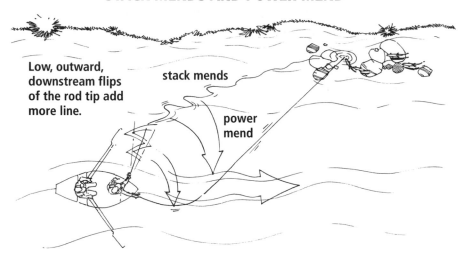

Low, outward, downstream flips of the rod tip add more line.

stack mends

power mend

After making a big or even exaggerated reach cast, flip extra feet of slack line toward the fly. These stack mends can give very long drag-free drifts for both dry flies and nymphs. Follow the fly's downstream progress with your rod tip.

Should a fish grab your fly sooner than expected during a stack mend, it can be difficult to set the hook. Try immediately making a huge mend or two toward midriver. This can not only set the hook, but the fly line now bellies downstream in the current, keeping the fish tight.

hooked, with the midriver currents dragging your line and keeping tension on the fish while you reel up on it until you make direct line contact. It's not foolproof, but it often works.

Tuck Casts

The aim of the tuck cast is to make the fly land before the line and leader. In addition to sinking your nymphs deeply, this allows longer drifts of a dry fly, especially in swirling bank eddies. It's achieved by overpowering the forward cast while keeping it a little higher over the water than usual (just like the

THE TUCK CAST AND TRIPLE HAUL

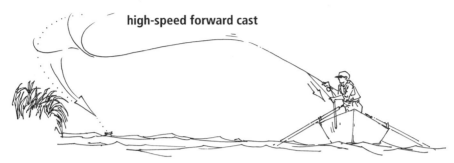

high-speed forward cast

An overpowered forward cast shot out at about shoulder level will turn line and fly over and then under the main length of your fly line. A tug or haul made with your line hand just as your fly is about to turn over will increase line speed and enhance the effect. Adding this third haul to a double-haul cast makes it a great wind-fighting tool. The triple haul both punches line out and helps force the fly down to the spot you were aiming for before the wind blows it away. Wind-resistant dry flies are hard to tuck, but any time you can get the fly to land before the leader and line do, it will improve your chances of fooling a trout.

bounce-back reach cast—the two can be combined). The line rapidly turns over, straightens, and then is carried by momentum to turn the fly under the main length of fly line. A fly can hit the water a second or two before the fly line falls, which can be just long enough to get an eddy fish to slurp it in. Big wind-resistant dry flies won't tuck as easily but a little tug or haul on the fly line, applied just as the forward cast begins to turn over and straighten, will accelerate line speed, enhancing the tuck.

Any time the fly lands before the line, or at least at the same time, you can get longer drifts. When a fly line slowly unfurls across the water with the fly landing last, the line will already be bellying downstream before the fly even hits the water. This effect is particularly noticeable in float fishing due to the swift currents nearest the angler and boat.

Another benefit of the tuck cast is that you can force a fly down with greater impact. This is useful when nymph-fishing. The added impetus helps sink a nymph all the quicker. The same goes for streamers. Some particularly ferocious trout will pounce on a streamer that's slapped down several feet from them (but not if it lands on their heads). That same forceful impact helps imitate hoppers, too. The splashdown can bring fish racing over to ingest. Real hoppers often land hard and from a high altitude; they can land anywhere across a big river. Others just tumble in from bankside grasses.

You can combine a tuck cast with a reach cast, too, although the act of reaching can pull the tuck right out of it. If you release slack through your rod's guides while reaching, some tuck can be maintained. This is an excellent way to fish bank eddies from the boat when casting at a downstream angle. The tuck cast will help presentations from all angles, though, and is worth practicing.

There are, of course, other casts and manipulations you can use when float-fishing, just as when wading. Sidearm casts might skip and sneak a fly under overhanging willows. Double- and triple-haul casts help shoot line farther faster and help keep it from getting blown away in a big wind. Hauling also takes a lot of work off your rod arm while helping to project flies high and safely above your boatmates.

On the whole, though, it's the slack-line reach cast that's the floating angler's most-used tool. Some regular mends will still be necessary to keep line from bellying and flies from dragging. One habitual good mend just after the line is laid out on a reach cast helps ensure a longer float.

Unsnagging a Fly from the Boat

One of those little tricks you can do with the line is unsnag a fly that's caught on a stream edge or shallow rock. It must be done as soon as the fly is snagged, before the boat floats any farther downstream. I call this tactic the unsnagging roll cast.

UNSNAGGING ROLL CAST

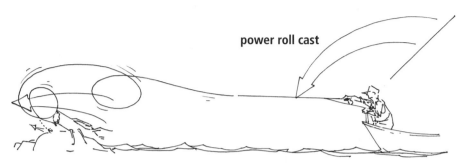

power roll cast

To unsnag a fly from rocks and logs, rip out some extra line from your reel. Throw one or more power roll casts up, over, and beyond the fly. When the fly line and leader go beyond the snag, pull back quickly. This will pull the fly from the opposite direction, often yanking it free. Do this immediately, before the boat drifts farther downstream. Don't do it if the fly is in bushes—just pull slowly but firmly and hope it comes out. Check the leader for frays.

First, rip a little extra line off your reel. Next, make an extra-powerful and high roll cast. The object is to propel your fly line and leader beyond your fly's position. It may take a couple of attempts to get your line up and far enough over the snag to do the trick. Ultimately, the roll cast goes beyond your fly and pulls it from behind, usually unsnagging it.

This technique doesn't work for flies tangled in bushes, however. The thing to do here is just to pull slowly and steadily on the line. The fly may creep its way out of the limbs. Any rash jerking of the line tends to worsen the situation or break off the fly. Always check your leader for frays after encounters with foliage, rocks, or other snags and after catching fish.

You may have to row over to undo some snags or perhaps just break off your fly. When rowing over to a snag, you may come to a point where it's difficult to continue to row because the bankside oar will have become incapacitated by the shore. The crawl stroke can be used to get closer than conventional rowing allows. If there are protruding bushes, they tend to get caught up in the bank oar, too. In areas of swift water, the angler may have just a second to unsnag the fly. The best procedure is to break off the limb that the fly is tangled on and extricate it at leisure in the boat. Watch your rod and line during this quick-grab operation. It's quite common for people to actually worsen the situation by concentrating on their fly while forgetting which way their rod is pointing. Their rod and fly line end up getting more tangled than the fly originally was. I see this all the time. Rods are occasionally broken, too. Put your rod down and point it the other way before going in to rescue your fly along a swift-water bank. Be careful not to snag the fly in your hand if the boat drifts off. You can also anchor near the snag and sometimes reach it from the boat; at other times, the angler must get out and walk. Make sure the location in which you stop is suitable for both anchoring and wading. I prefer to break my fly off rather than interrupt the other anglers and make more work for the rower. Always bring a good supply of flies, and expect to lose some along the way.

DRY-FLY, NYMPH, AND STREAMER TECHNIQUES

A day on the river is likely to present anglers with ever-changing opportunities, each requiring different tactics. Pre- and post-hatch nymphing and streamer fishing can take up much of the day. Plentiful hatches can bring on sessions of dry-fly sight fishing. Pre-rigging rods for each tactic saves downtime on the stream. Being skilled in all techniques is a big plus, as is having the mindset to adapt.

Many anglers today carry a dedicated nymph rod, plus a dry-fly rod and perhaps a third streamer rod. It's a lot faster to just switch rods than it is to re-rig. Newer boats have built-in rod tubes to protect them, but usually don't have room for more than three for each fisher.

At the beginning of the day, or when no one technique stands out as the best, the two casters should try different methods. It's best for the bow angler to use dry flies or light nymph rigs, which are less likely to spook fish on the drop, giving the stern angler more hope for his offering. (The two anglers usually switch positions during the day.) The stern angler can follow up with a heavier nymph rig or streamer, both of which tend to splash down with a little more impact. Systematically cover different feed lanes, too. Giving fish some variety is a good way to start. Hopefully, it won't be long before you ascertain the trout's preference.

Lack of success calls for fly or water type changes, or for adding more weight to the leader. (You know the old saying, "The difference between a good nympher and a great one is a split shot.") If you had to bet on one technique out of the gate (in lieu of rising fish), it would be deep nymphing with two varying nymphs.

I always hope for some response to dry flies, though, and prefer to fish a dry fly with a nymph dropper. This is especially true from the bow, where you can lay a long prospecting cast out ahead of the boat. Adjust the nymph dropper length to match water depth. All the while, keep glancing ahead and all across the river for rising fish. As river structure changes, time passes, and hatches commence, more fly changes are likely to be needed. Wind, cloud cover, and temperature variations may also call for increased experimentation. Again, run the more delicate landing technique off the bow. Sitting to cast in the bow is also less likely to scare fish, leaving more for the stern angler.

Dry-Fly Fishing for Trout

The old-school float fisherman's game centered largely around dry-fly fishing. Whether casting to a sighted trout or getting hits

FISHING FROM SLOW WATER INTO FAST

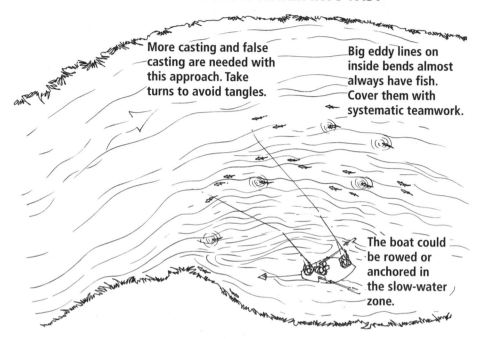

More casting and false casting are needed with this approach. Take turns to avoid tangles.

Big eddy lines on inside bends almost always have fish. Cover them with systematic teamwork.

The boat could be rowed or anchored in the slow-water zone.

When the boat is in slower water and the target area in swifter water, a change in casting angles is called for. Instead of the downstream reach cast, anglers should use the upstream approach, as when wade-fishing. Cast upstream, strip in line as the fly floats back toward you, and be ready for a grab. This can apply to dry flies, nymphs, or streamers.

out of the blue while prospecting, it's the take that many love to see.

Anglers could disembark and wade-fish, but some places are too deep or have tall bank-side bushes that make wade-fishing tough. In big eddies, waders sometimes kick up enough silt (which settles in eddies) to put fish down, since that water recirculates.

First you must constantly look ahead, both for rising fish and for likely pockets, drop-offs, and bank edges. The bow angler has the visual advantage here, even over the rower. He can also alert the rower to rowing hazards, as the bow angler's body can block the rower's view. Glance back and forth from your fly to the next spot you might want to hit. You are progressing downstream and will need to be efficient to cover it all. Speed casters with minimum downtime catch more trout. Modern fly rods are capable of throwing casts with far greater line speed than most anglers realize. Quicker casts, especially with dry flies, result in far less wasted time, better air-dried flies, and lessen the chance of trout seeing your fly line in the air. The two casters work as a team for maximum inner-lane and outer-lane coverage.

Traditional small-stream fishermen keep wanting to look back upstream. Get over that impulse! Look ahead, master the reach cast, and be able to cast fairly far. You have to cast beyond the "fear zone," a certain diameter around the boat in

There are many anchored situations where casting back upstream will be just like wade fishing. Being in the boat can be a plus in tricky wading spots and helps keep your line higher above bankside vegetation.

TROUT SPOTS BEGINNERS IGNORE

extreme shallows

Trout like shallow water. If not bothered, they'll sit in water that just barely covers their backs. They can nymph or rise in the same spot. The entire feeding universe is compressed into a 6-inch zone!

upstream of islands

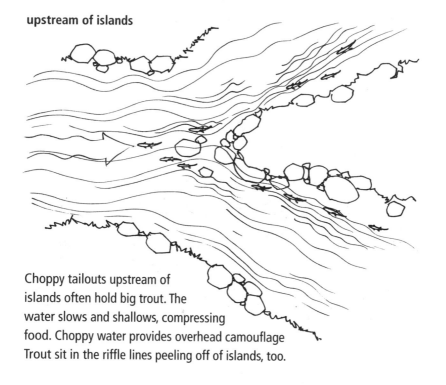

Choppy tailouts upstream of islands often hold big trout. The water slows and shallows, compressing food. Choppy water provides overhead camouflage Trout sit in the riffle lines peeling off of islands, too.

upstream of obstructions

Beginners often think that trout only hold behind rocks. In fact, fish will often hold in the pillow of quiet water upstream of obstructions where they can clearly see all the food coming.

midriver foam lanes

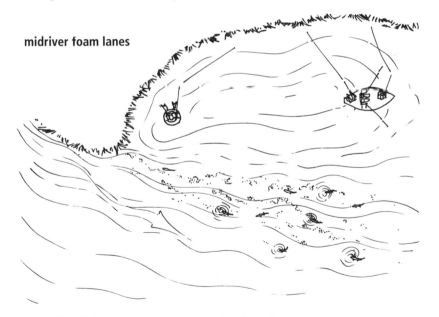

Some float fishermen get too obsessed with banks. In slow water, trout may be rising in foam lanes that spread way out across midriver. The rower in particular should be looking for risers in every direction.

DRY-FLY BOAT ANGLES

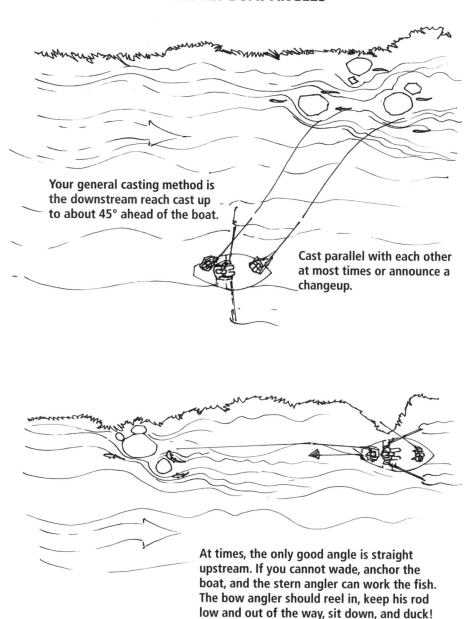

Your general casting method is the downstream reach cast up to about 45° ahead of the boat.

Cast parallel with each other at most times or announce a changeup.

At times, the only good angle is straight upstream. If you cannot wade, anchor the boat, and the stern angler can work the fish. The bow angler should reel in, keep his rod low and out of the way, sit down, and duck!

**Rower holds the oars as downstream rudders
to stop the boat from swinging.**

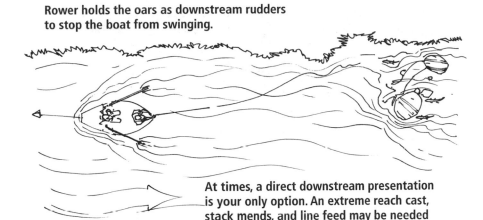

At times, a direct downstream presentation
is your only option. An extreme reach cast,
stack mends, and line feed may be needed
to sneak the fly to the fish. Rest the fish
between casts, as you have to pull the line
back up by him on a refusal.

which your craft's presence scares trout. Anglers standing in
the bow scare trout at a greater distance than do sitting ones.
Fish can also spook from seeing your line in the air or from the
spray your false casts shower down on flat water.

At times, you'll want to pull the boat in and anchor just
downstream of trout, especially in big eddies and riffle lines
with defined current seams. Here, the stern angler can shoot
casts back upstream to rising fish from the boat as long as the
bow angler sits down or ducks. Along deep banks, this may
be the only option. The boat's position just offshore can help
keep your backcast out of the willows. On shallower stretches,
both anglers can disembark, wade, and fish for these trout.
Indeed, some anglers prefer to use the boat mainly as transportation and to wade-fish much of the day. Keep track of your
time and mileage, though. Anglers commonly stay too long in
spots and have to row out in the dark on unfamiliar water.

As previously mentioned, the 45-degree forward reach cast
is your primary technique for fishing dry flies from a boat. A

Some anglers prefer to use the boat mostly as transportation, disembarking to wade-fish much of the best water. The longer the float, however, the more time you will spend in the boat—unless you want to take out after dark.

crisp 8 ½- to 9-foot, 4- to 6-weight fly rod can throw 60 feet of weight-forward line easily. Double-hauling during the cast will speed up your presentation and make your casts longer, allowing you to cover more water, more efficiently. Another benefit of the double haul is that it can reduce the work done by your rod arm up to 30 percent. This is a lot of energy saved over the course of a day. The added speed of a double haul also dries off your flies better, making them float higher.

I often have anglers in my boat fish two dry flies at a time. The first fly is larger, so anglers can see it. It mimics the larger hatch that would be appealing to trout that day. The second fly is usually smaller, and sometimes very small, fished on lighter tippet. It imitates the tiny insects trout sometimes prefer. Note that tiny aquatic insects usually hatch in much greater numbers, and for longer periods, than do big flies, for weeks or

TWO DRY FLIES

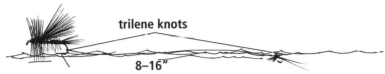

trilene knots

8–16"

Fish a large fly that you can see and a smaller one to match the hatch. I keep a small barb on the hook of the large fly so the dropper can't slide off.

DRY FLY AND EMERGER

8–16"

A dry fly with a subsurface emerger can up the catch rate with picky fish. The dry fly should match the largest available insect or terrestrial.

DRY FLY AND NYMPH

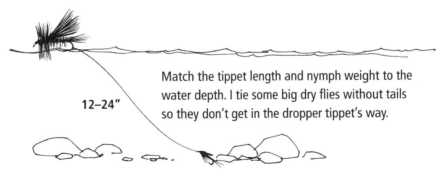

12–24"

Match the tippet length and nymph weight to the water depth. I tie some big dry flies without tails so they don't get in the dropper tippet's way.

months instead of just days. Consequently, at times trout will focus on the little ones, those an angler has a hard time seeing from the boat. The second fly might be a midge, spentwing, microcaddis, surface emerger, or a nymph.

Leader and tippet are of great importance, too. Big flies like Golden Stones and hoppers fish best on 3X, or even 2X when in riffles and wind-chopped water, but for today's heavily fished

TRILENE KNOT

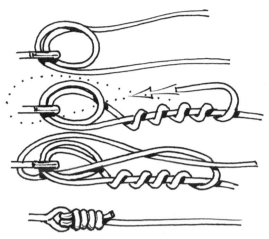

1. Go through the eye of the fly twice.

2. Wrap the tag end 3 to 4 times around the leader.

3. Put the tag end through both eye loops and then the big loop.

4. Moisten and smoothly tighten.

The trilene knot is one of the strongest fly knots you can use. Going twice around the eye spreads the line stress and prevents the knot from slipping.

and leader-shy trout, the lightest tippet you can get away with will up your catch rate. For medium-size caddis and larger mayflies I use 4X and 5X on flat water. Smaller #16-18s require 5X and on slicks, I use 6X for #18-22s. On the Missouri River, we have some large, fast fish and big weed beds. Tippet lighter than 6X tends to break off. Your situation might make 7X or 8X workable. You do need to moderate your hook set with light tippets. Just snug up on the line; don't give them the tarpon slam.

I like to have two types of fly floatant on hand: the liquid type (one that doesn't gel in cold weather) to use on fresh flies and the powdered dry-fly crystals to resurrect sodden flies that refuse to float. Dry sodden flies as well as you can and then shake them in the crystals to make them float like new.

For strength, I prefer the triple surgeon's knot (using three turns) for leader to tippet and the trilene knot to the fly (and also fly-to-fly droppers). These are about as strong as you can get. Retie flies after a couple of fish—knots tend to weaken. Feel the leader for frays, too.

Dry-Fly Accuracy

A simple trick you can use to increase your accuracy is to skid a fly into the correct feed lane. Cast down and across and try to get the fly beyond a rising trout's feed lane. Then lift the rod tip high and swing it back upstream (similar to reaching) until the fly skids into the trout's lane. When it gets to the lane, lower the rod tip near the water and point it toward the fly. This gives a long-enough drag-free float to fool many trout. The skid should take place just before the fly is in the trout's view, say, 4 to 6 feet upstream of it. This should produce a dead drift of 10 feet or so, enough to do the job and do it well. Naturally, a fly that floats well—one that doesn't routinely sink when skidded—aids the process.

You can use the skid in other situations, too—to lengthen the drag-free drift of a hopper, attractor dry, or indicator nymph. When a fly starts swinging and dragging at the end of your initial presentation, and if it's still going over a premium zone, a lift, reach, and skid will rejuvenate the dead drift for a little while longer. You can do it repeatedly if your fly keeps floating.

You might have a fly drifting out near the bank and then see a trout rise to your side of it. A quick skid can line up your fly with the feed lane without a recast. Such little manipulations of rod, line, and fly come in handy for many things.

Nymphing

Deep nymphing from a boat is extremely effective. The biggest rowing difference when nymphing is that you want to float at current speed, not slow the boat down a lot as when dry-fly fishing. Floating at current speed allows nymphs to sink deeply and stay down in front of trout for a long time. Minimize down-

NYMPHING ROW-AROUNDS

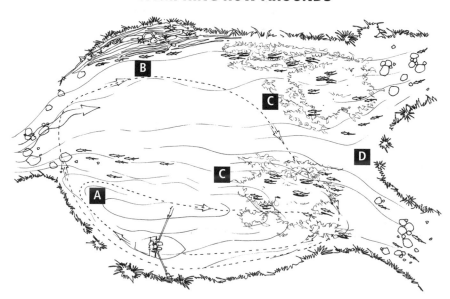

Big tailwater rivers have a lot of widespread trout. The rower uses the slow side of the river to row back upstream and fish productive zones again. Follow the inner dashed route to fish the big eddy line **A** that peels off the point (always an area where a lot of trout hold) before hitting the weed bed flats at **C**. Weed-bed flats of 2 to 5 feet hold numerous scattered fish. The outer dashed route ferries over to a steep bank, where fish are lined up tight at **B**. Then you'll hit more weed-bed flats **C**, and the productive tailout upstream of an island **D**.

time, and maximize fish time. (Downtime includes excessive casting, indecision over fly selection, and tangles, which are common when you're flinging a strike indicator, split shot, and multiple nymphs.) When nymphing, you want a little extra slack on the water to ward off drag, but not so much that you can't set the hook.

Since floating at current speed works best, row-arounds have become a popular tactic. After nymphing through a prom-

Deep nymphers target midriver drop-offs, weed bed flats, converging currents, foam lines, and the like. Such water is usually 2 to 6 feet deep. Strike indicators, split shot, and a two-nymph rig are commonly employed.

ising eddy line or weed-bed flat, the boatman ferries over to the slow side of the river, rows back upstream, and floats the route again. Some guides will keep doing this as long as it catches fish. They'll make subtle drift-lane variations in order to systematically cover the entire bottom. A lot of boats doing rowarounds have a circus ride look. Avoid wading anglers and other boats, though. Some rowers have no sense of how close is too close.

Deep-nymphing trout can live all across the river. Whereas many dry-fly boaters concentrate on banks and shallow riffles, deep nymphers cover far-spreading eddy lines and midstream weed flats. Target water 2 to 6 feet deep, including giant eddies, midriver bars, and tailouts. Trout in deep water don't care if the boat floats right over them.

NYMPH RIG

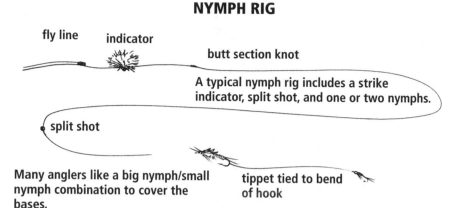

fly line   indicator

butt section knot

A typical nymph rig includes a strike indicator, split shot, and one or two nymphs.

split shot

Many anglers like a big nymph/small nymph combination to cover the bases.

tippet tied to bend of hook

I'll usually put the indicator and split shot above a knot so they can't slide down the leader. I prefer triple surgeon's knots for leader-tippet connections, and trilene knots for attaching tippet to fly.

When float fishing, it is important to carry strike indicators, split shot, and nymphs with various weights (from none to tungsten beads). The strike indicator distance above the flies will be adjusted to water depth. When floating, though, the depth changes so often that you usually pick a middle-ground distance, say, 6 feet. In addition to San Juan Worms, scuds, and sow bugs, I stock an assortment of stonefly nymphs, mayfly nymphs, and caddis and midge larvae, plus emergers.

If you want to catch fish, fear not the bobber. I always keep an eye open for risers, though.

Streamer Fishing

Banging out streamers from the boat is good clean fun. Day-dreams of big browns swim between the ears. Trout like all kinds of shorelines—those with obvious cover, and slow, boring-looking ones without. In the cold water of late winter to early spring, trout can gang up in slow, deep water where they don't have to fight the current. In warmer months, they spread into

CASTING IN OVALS

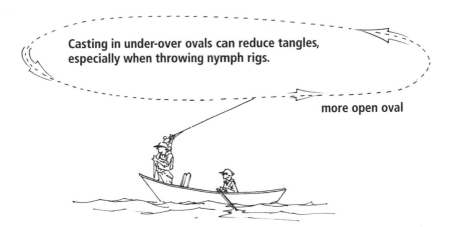

Casting in under-over ovals can reduce tangles, especially when throwing nymph rigs.

more open oval

Smooth, non-jerky power is what you need for multi-piece nymph rigs. Keep casts well above your boatmates' heads!

When dry-fly fishing, cast tighter ovals at higher speeds. Most good casters don't cast back and forth on the same plane (as is often thought); they cast in tight ovals.

faster runs and extreme shallows. (This is part metabolism and part food availability.) The streamer can sweep it all.

Most streamer casts will be straight into the bank. Trout also seem to like a slight upstream cast thrown a little behind the boat. These angles help present your fly broadside to the fish and make it look like a floundering baitfish. Trout, small trout, and baitfish often live in close proximity. When little fish are healthy and quick, trout generally won't spend the energy to chase them down. Should one be injured or floundering, though, trout pounce right on them.

Drop the streamer near the bank, strip once, and pause to let it sink a bit. Then begin a strip–pause–strip retrieve. When trout are less aggressive, including when water is icy cold, they may take mostly on the pauses. In that case, slow it down

CASTING STREAMERS TO BANKS

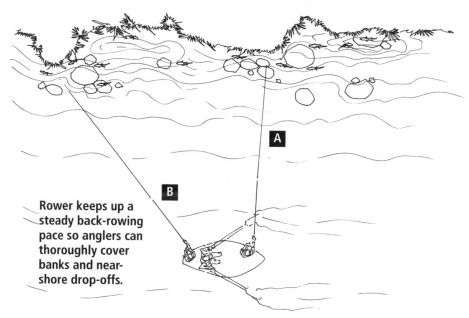

Rower keeps up a steady back-rowing pace so anglers can thoroughly cover banks and near-shore drop-offs.

A. The standard streamer angle is straight into the bank. You can still use a reach cast so the faster water near the boat doesn't belly the line downstream so quickly. Then point the rod at the fly and keep it low to the water while stripping. You can feel takes and set the hook better this way. Use 1X to 3X tippet.

B. Trout also like a presentation that is angled upstream. This gives a down and across, floundering baitfish look. Take turns casting, though, as your backcasts may no longer be parallel and can easily tangle.

more; watch for follows, and even dead-drift it with twitches. When temperatures are ideal and the fish are "on," they'll take it every which way. Quicker stripping that covers more water can be the ticket.

Continue using a reach cast with streamers, so the faster water near the boat doesn't belly the line downstream too quickly. Mend as needed. Then keep the rod tip low, pointed at

Banging out streamers to likely bank water is a favorite Western pastime.
Preferred angles include directly sideways into the bank and slightly back
upstream. Both give a floundering baitfish look. Strips and pauses give
motion and opportunities for trout to pounce.

FISHING STREAMERS MIDRIVER

Anglers at B and C cast upstream, mend, allow the streamer to sink, and then strip or sweep it downstream and across the river.

Boat at A is still in fast water. Anglers use 45° reach cast forward.

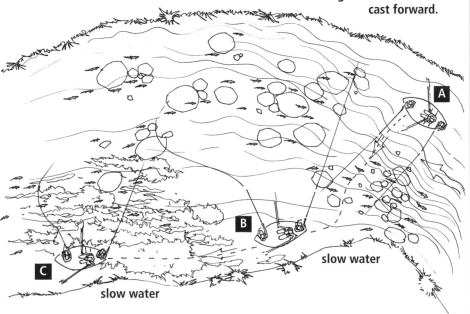

slow water

slow water

A. The rower starts in midriver, hits the productive inside eddy line, and then ferries near the bank to hit midriver grooves.
B. The rower uses the crawl stroke parallel to the bank while the anglers fish a midstream boulder lane. Ideally you can keep the boat offshore just enough to keep backcasts out of the foliage. You can fish here as you would when wading. Take turns casting.
C. On broad weed bed flats and tailouts, trout can be widespread. Cast far and fish all the way back to the boat. If a trout follows but doesn't take, try a long pause in your stripping.

the fly, and begin stripping. You'll feel takes better with the rod tip low, almost on the water. Use 1X to 3X tippet, though. A streamer strip meeting the take of a bold big fish can break light tippet.

Banks aren't the only streamer targets. Boulders, gravel bar drop-offs, weed bed flats, and midstream runs could all beg for a cast. At times, it's better for the rower to creep along the bank using the crawl stroke, while sweeping streamers through the middle of the river. On broad weed bed flats, throw streamers far, and strip them all the way back to the boat. This is much

Line control is critical in the fast-paced game of stripping and shooting line while fishing streamers. Many pontoon boats have built-in stripping baskets to prevent tangles. MARK LISK PHOTO COURTESY OF OUTCAST SPORTING GEAR

like wade-fishing, but the boat gives you an elevated position, which can help in throwing backcasts over streamside foliage. It also keeps you moving along if you have miles to go. Steelhead and salmon can be fished in this manner. Sink tip lines might be needed here.

In shallower rivers, streamers can be fished with floating lines, which make it easier to mend and quickly pick up line for the next cast. Add split shot to the leader for additional weight.

High-density sink-tip lines can be a good option for deeper water. Full sinking lines can have applications but aren't used much. Pulling one up out of the water is tedious, and mends have no effect. Low backcasts due to line and streamer weight are dangerous for others in the boat. If you do fish a full sinking line, strip it all the way in before backcasting so you can cast the heavy line safely above your boatmates' heads.

When trout are really on, streamers bring out their predatory instincts. Big browns and rainbows are the end results.

RELEASING FISH

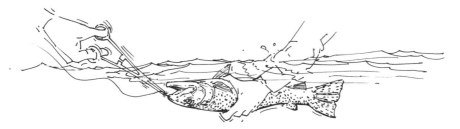

To unhook and release fish, keep them underwater, turned belly up. This usually pacifies them, making them easy to work with. I use my fingers to unhook flies when I can, since they are less damaging to small flies. Use hemostats for harder to reach or firmly embedded flies. If you're going to take a photo, have the cameraman ready, shoot quickly, and get the fish back in the water.

Streamer color is subjective. I know good anglers who use black, brown, olive, tan, yellow, chartreuse, and white, all with success. Each has a favorite. Most of the trout's natural food is camouflaged with the bottom. Commonly ingested items include crayfish, sculpin, leeches, and minnows, in about that order. Yet trout on the prowl will take unnaturally bright streamers, including flashy white, yellow, and chartreuse.

We'll often fish two streamers at once, experimenting with different colors. Trout more often take the second streamer, since they tend to follow them before grabbing. If they take the first one repeatedly, they prefer that color. Two rods banging double streamers can really cover some water.

A smooth-feeding reel is a good asset for hot-running fish, though it's often more important when wading than when fishing from a boat, for following the fish with the boat increases the odds of landing it. Deep-water fish tend to dive. Shallow-water fish zoom sideways.

TACTICS FOR OTHER SPECIES
Smallmouth Bass

Smallmouth are widespread across the Appalachians from Tennessee on up to Maine. Great Lakes tributaries have plenty. There are West Coast populations north of San Francisco, and even in Montana we have a few. The rivers they live in are a lot like trout rivers in nature: scenic, semiswift, and rocky, with ledges, boulders, and bars. Smallmouth often feed the same way as trout. They lurk in eddies, along current seams, in the shade of trees, and around rock piles. They're ready to get on everything from mayfly hatches to their favorite, crayfish. Smallmouth are a great float-fishing target through much of the season. They fight like crazy and can greatly expand your geographic horizons.

Smallmouth are cool-water fish (unlike largemouth), most active when water temperatures are about 60 to 65 degrees. It's then that they hit poppers, sliders, and dry flies with attitude. Late spring, early summer, and toward fall can be best. Summer heat can slow down midday fish, except in their northernmost range. The cooler, low-light hours might then prove best.

Smallmouth love to lurk around rocks and ledges, where moderate currents, eddies, and cover coincide. Here they find crayfish, hellgrammites, minnows, and nymphs to fill up on. They also occupy shady spots, banks of the right depths, and tailouts. Water that's 1 to 4 feet deep makes up a lot of your target area, pocketwater of the prettiest sort.

Smallmouth rivers can be big or small (they live in lakes, too). Many offer great float-fishing potential and beautiful scenery. The rowing techniques, anchoring, and fishing strategies will feel familiar to big-river trout fishermen. Only a slight change of equipment might be in order. The poppers, sliders, Clousers, and crayfish used can call for a bump up in rod weight. A good 6 to 7 weight will do, and some prefer 8 weights.

Smallmouth bass offer lots of scenic float-fishing opportunities around the country. They're good fighters and are somewhat troutlike in their feeding behavior.

Weight-forward floating fly lines help bomb out heavy or air-resistant flies. A short sink-tip is useful for boulder base dredging with streamers. Use leaders of 7 to 9 feet, tapering from 1X to 4X. Set the hook a little harder than you would on a 5X trout. Smallmouth have tougher mouths. Be ready for a reaction!

While floating, the bow angler can shoot the nearer eddies, while the stern caster picks farther pockets, ledge drops, shadows, and banks. Remember to cast parallel with each other and a bit forward of the boat. Reach casts still apply. Taking turns at casting avoids tangles.

The bow angler could try dry flies, Dahlberg Divers, poppers, and such, while the stern angler experiments with bottom-bouncing streamers. If and when a definite preference is established, both anglers can adopt that technique. There are

From Oregon's John Day to the Susquehanna in Pennsylvania, many anglers target smallies from a wide variety of watercraft.

times when fast retrieves work best. Other days, slow-fished ones with long pauses do better. Smallmouth can be moody and picky. Figuring out their whims is part of the river day.

Little smallmouth often school up around good river structure and eddies. Large ones tend to be more solitary. If all you're catching is little guys, try bumping up your fly size. You might also want to try fishing a little deeper. Big ones are usually out there but, as always, are harder to come by. They may wait for the low-light periods of dawn and dusk to come on strong, especially in the hottest part of summer. Fly type, color, size, depth, and action can all make a difference on any given day.

From Maryland to Maine, Oregon to the Ozarks, and all around the Great Lakes states, smallmouth wait to pounce. Some anglers cash in after their best trout fishing of the season is over. Others target smallmouth prime times on scenic rivers around the country. Add them to you list of float-fishing must-dos.

Salmon and Steelhead

Big fish are a big deal to most anglers. Salmon and steelhead (and also lake-run browns) get them fired up. Rain, cold, and discomfort will all be tolerated when a run is on. Work, household duties, and maintenance issues might all be shunned. (Unfortunately, etiquette is sometimes shunned, too. The bigger the fish, the narrower the focus.)

Traditional West Coast float fishing features boats with one or two spin fishermen in the bow and none in the stern. The boat slowly rows over deep fish holds, back-trolling diving plugs, big spoons, or bait. Heads and bellies of pools, up and downstream of boulders, along drop-offs, in big circulating eddies, and across giant tailouts—all are dredged. Row-arounds can be used to rework eddies and runs. Many of these are canyon rivers, where rapids, runs, and pools alternate.

Others, particularly fly fishermen, just use the boat as transportation to and from good wade-fishing runs. Salmon and steelhead tend to use the same lies in a river, generation after generation (until changed by floods or rockslides). In bright daylight, they tend to lay low and deep, or under the cover of broken, choppy water. They like the feel of some current in their faces, but not too much of it. They do most of their upstream migrating in the dark hours.

Anglers systematically wade-fish known fish-holding water and at times sight fish there. They might work a run with one fly or technique, walk back upstream, and try it again with another. Traditionally, the wet-fly swing was used. This has been supplemented by dead drifts, skating dry flies, and deep nymphing. Bottom-bouncing an egg pattern can be as good as anything. Realistic nymphs are often plied.

The two salmon-steelhead arenas are the West Coast from San Francisco north and the Great Lakes tributaries (which also feature some huge lake-run browns). West Coast rivers vary in size and nature. Some flow through beautiful rain forests. Others ease through fertile farm valleys. Many rush down the coastal mountain ranges and are big, swift, and potentially dangerous, with plenty of rapids. Heavy winter rains have to be worked around and can bring rivers up to tremendous levels fast. Big-water boats and serious rowing skills can be required, along with good judgment. Longer fly and Spey rods are favored, as some giant runs are there. Steelhead start up the rivers in September and remain into spring. They can hold a little shallower than salmon, in as little as a few feet of broken water (which serves as overhead camouflage). Salmon runs go from April to late fall, with king or chinook salmon coming first and silvers a bit later. They can be quite deep in places. Run timing varies from river to river as you head north up the coast. It's possible to catch one of these migratory fish at almost any time of year.

Great Lakes tributaries are mostly smaller, mellower, and often best covered by wade-fishing. Lighter rods and lines are sometimes used, fishing to twitchy sighted fish. Some Great Lakes rivers are open during spawning season, and it's legal to sight-fish spawners on their shallow redds (primarily in quickening tailouts, where finer gravel settles). On West Coast rivers, fishing to wild spawners is either illegal (closed season) or discouraged.

When float-fishing long miles of salmon or steelhead rivers, you can use a ploy that's a lot like wade-fishing in application but keeps some forward progress going. (Some western rivers have very slippery boulders, too, making wading a chore.) Row the boat off to the side of productive-looking holding water, using the crawl stroke close in to shore. These fish aren't as bank oriented as trout, so floating the edges and fishing the middle or edges of the main current can work well. One of two basic techniques is commonly used: the classic wet-fly swing or weighted nymphing. The wet-fly swing also includes skating or waking flies for steelhead. Use a big down-and-across cast (to mostly across), with a giant reach cast built in. You might need

When steelhead fishing, most fly fishers use a boat to get from one spot to the next.

an additional big mend or two at the beginning, too. Allow the wet fly to sink awhile, before the current tightens the line and the fly begins to swing. Follow the fly's progress downstream and bankward with the rod tip, eventually paralleling the shore. The idea is to create a slow, even swing of the fly across the river. Additional mends and even line feed can be used to slow it down and keep it submerged. (Skidding and waking flies don't want to go too fast either.)

The two casters do this in a systematic way. Let the bow rod get started. Shortly after his cast, the stern rod follows suit. Keep the two lines in sync for better coverage and less tangling. You can experiment with different flies, distances, weighting (if any), colors, and subtle action. The wet-fly swing has been used successfully for centuries on European and North American salmon rivers. Besides being a proven West Coast steelhead method, it also works for trout. Floating lines are traditionally

DEEP NYMPHING FROM A BOAT

Deep nymphers ignore the shallow banks that dry-fly anglers like.

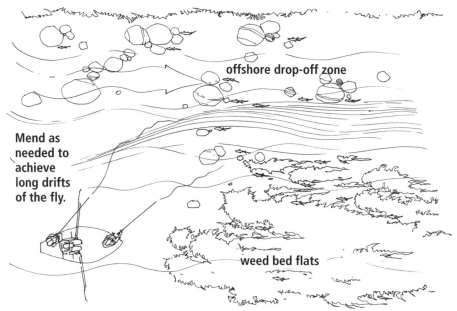

offshore drop-off zone

**Mend as
needed to
achieve
long drifts
of the fly.**

weed bed flats

Take turns casting slightly downstream with a reach cast. Leave a little extra slack on the water to eliminate drag, but not so much that you can't set the hook right away. The boat floats at the indicator's speed, instead of slowing down. Set the hook as soon as the indicator moves. By then, the fish has already had the nymph for a second or two and is already trying to shake it out. In deep water, fish don't mind the boat much and can be caught quite close to it.

used, but sink-tip and specialty high-density sinking lines have a place (especially for deeper-holding salmon).

There are times and places where this doesn't work so well. Some Great Lakes tributaries and deep western salmon holds do better with nymphing techniques. In this case, weighted nymphs and egg patterns are cast upstream at a 45-degree angle or so, mended or stack mended, and dead-drifted along the bottom. This is a wade-fishing application done from a slow-crawling boat. The boat crawls the shoreline (or outer grooves), while the two anglers deep-nymph likely spots. Some fish are sighted, others imagined in prime holding lies. You want the longest drifts you can get, so the nymph has time to get and stay deep. It is often necessary to make additional mends and feed line into the drift to cover the water effectively. When your line begins to belly at the end, let it swing a bit before recasting. Salmon and steelhead may take a nymph on the uplifting swing.

Most good runs should be worked slowly and thoroughly. Anadromous fish are not always forthcoming on the first drift. A row-around, or even walking the boat back upstream to refloat, might be in order, as holding water can be spread laterally across the river. Fish can be in zones that are too deep to wade. They're not all lined up in a row either. Start with the nearest grooves and then go back up and drift the farther ones. Keep nymphs near the bottom and drag free. Use as much weight as it takes, as well as a strike indicator to denote the sometimes subtle takes. Salmon and steelhead can just mouth the fly. It's not necessarily like a big brown or smallmouth whacking it.

Use 7- to 9-weight rods and 0X to 3X tippet for the wet-fly method. A big fish take on tight line can part company on too light a leader. Even here, though, salmon and steelhead often mouth the fly in a nonaggresive, porpoising manner. A major school of thought suggests that you don't set the hook in a quick, troutish way. Instead, you do nothing and let the weight and downward impulse of the fish hook itself, hopefully back in the tough corner of its mouth. Too quick a hook set just yanks the fly from its half-open maw.

Nymph fishing often uses lighter rods and leaders, down to 4X. Lighter leader sinks more quickly since there's less water resistance. On some heavily fished Great Lakes rivers, shallow-water fish are spooky, too. Light leaders and bottom-bouncing

SALMON AND STEELHEAD RUNS

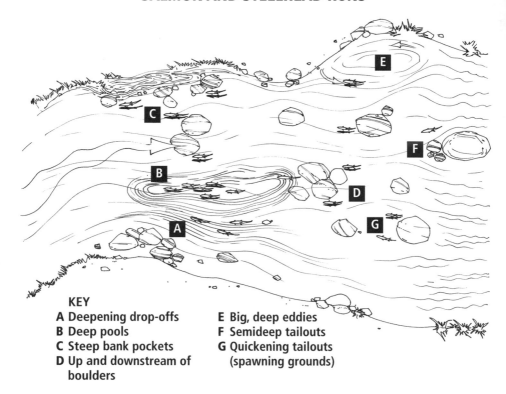

KEY

A Deepening drop-offs
B Deep pools
C Steep bank pockets
D Up and downstream of boulders

E Big, deep eddies
F Semideep tailouts
G Quickening tailouts (spawning grounds)

Steelhead and salmon are less bank-oriented than trout. They seek sanctuary and current breaks on their way upstream.

Traditional plug- and bait-fishing boats row over the fish, back trolling (from the front of the boat only). Deep fish don't care much.

Fly and spin fishers float to the slow side, working up and across, sideways, and then down and across. Row-arounds are possible here, too.

egg patterns fool more sighted fish. Match your hook set to the leader strength and hold on! You may have to chase them on light tackle, either on foot or in the boat. Too long a line out can spell disaster if a lot of boulders and downfall trees are around. A shorter, controlled line ups your odds of landing them.

Remember, though, shorter lines have less stretch and give. Be ready to let fish run line off the reel at a moment's notice. Have an oversized net on board to land them.

White and Hickory Shad

Shad run up the rivers of both coasts from April to mid-May (and as early as February on Florida's St. Johns River). As harbingers of spring, they arrive with dogwood and cherry blossoms. After a long winter, this attracts throngs of anglers to productive spots. Water temperatures of 55 to 60 degrees are key to their arrival. A big cold front can slow them down.

Shad average 1½ to 6 pounds. White (American) shad are the larger and more desired of the two species, with females being larger than males. Female white shad can approach 8 pounds. They fight hard for their size, making them a good fly-rod and light-tackle fish. White shad dig deep and use the current. Hickory shad can jump quite a bit.

Since shad run upstream to spawn, finding a school of them is key. They won't be everywhere, but they'll gang up at the right spots. Long, swift, deepish runs with gravel bottoms are best. The heads and tails of pools and runs are their gathering spots. Bottom structure in the belly of a pool can add more good real estate, as can deep banks. Shad will fin in deeper tails of pools to rest and while away the bright daylight hours. They may push up to the heads of runs just before dark, getting ready to run upstream. Low-light periods fish best, including dawn, dusk, overcast days, and in dark shadows.

Boats can be of great advantage, both for traveling the river to find hot spots (which aren't usually a secret) and to keep offshore enough to clear your backcast. Some places are tough wading, too. Much of the fishing will be done while anchored, for once you find a school of shad, you should stick with it. Cast upstream, mend, let the line and fly sink, and then swing it across the targeted run. If the fishing slows down, try differ-

Shad fishing is popular on the West and East Coasts. Boats often allow anglers to get to the prime water. CHIP O'BRIEN PHOTO

ent fly or shad dart colors before leaving. The fish can be picky about color, depth, and action, which can change over time. It's likely that they're still there.

Fly rod tackle for shad should be heavy enough to cast far, cover a lot of water, and at times throw high-density sinking lines. A good 7 to 8 weight will do. Depending on your location and timing, full sinking, sink tip, or lighter floating lines might work (even down to 4 weights). As the fish can be nervous, 3X to 4X tippet is fine. Hickory shad may take closer to the surface in low evening light, as they get agitated to migrate. Big white shad can hit hard, run like mad in a current, and break too light a tippet if all goes wrong.

Streamers and Clousers for shad are typically small, #6 to #10, brightly colored, and sometimes sparse. Bright white and fluorescent colors (often tied with tinsel shanks) work best. Yellows, oranges, reds, and chartreuse are popular. One color may outproduce all others for any given day, light condition, or water clarity. In the light-tackle spinning realm, shad darts are popular and productive. These small jigs in the colors just mentioned are often fished two at a time, in tandem. You can do that with streamers, too, but keep your backcasts high over the boat.

There are inland shad and shadlike species to target as well. In the Ohio and Tennessee river systems, golden shad run. Come April, these Tennessee tarpon of 1 to 3 pounds head upstream below big dams. (They're also used for big catfish bait.) Good locations include the French Broad and Clinch rivers. Like all shad, they're numerous and fight hard for their size.

Out west, in the lower Missouri and Yellowstone, roam hordes of goldeyes. These only run about 12 inches, maxing out at 2 pounds. Though not a true shad, they have that look, plus a large yellow eye (hence the name). Riffle drop-offs and the heads of pools feature schools of goldeyes on these semiturbid rivers. They fight and jump like crazy for their size, rise freely to mayfly and caddis hatches, and add life to these lonely prairie outposts. You might be the only one on the river! They'll hit almost anything with gusto and are a great fish for kids and beginners to practice on. Early summer is prime, after runoff, from late June into August.

Trout and shad in spring, smallmouth from summer till fall, and salmon and steelhead into winter—that will keep your rowing muscles tuned!

6

Choosing and Outfitting the Right Boat

S electing a river boat is no simple matter these days. A growing industry is supplying recreational craft in more designs, sizes, materials, and prices than ever before.

A prospective buyer has much to consider based on the water and wind conditions where he lives and plans to fish. Whitewater maneuvering demands, wind frequency and ferocity, the number of people one plans to fish with, storage capabilities, fishing comfort and stability, and price range are among the major considerations. Storage, transport options, and the quality or even presence of boat ramps on local waters bear some thought, too. An occasional floater might prefer the trunk-loading and easier storage option of a midgrade raft or personal watercraft. The hard-core frequent-floating addict tends to like the trailered readiness of a slick-rigged drift boat (which can cost upwards of $8,000 these days). Let's consider some of the options.

RAFT, PRAM, OR DRIFT BOAT?
Rafts
There are many makes and models of inflatables, or rafts, to choose from, most from 8 to 18 feet in length. Prices currently

Raft packages can include front and rear knee braces, anchor systems, comfortable seats, and drop-in coolers. Shop around for the best size, price, and features to suit your fishing.

range from about $2,000 to $6,000. You get what you pay for. Most fishermen prefer 12- to 14-foot boats. Experienced boaters and quality boat manufacturers speak of rafts in terms of feet in length and width and tube diameter, not as six- or eight-person rafts or what have you. Midsized rafts are easy to row, have acceptable room and storage capabilities, and will handle most any river situation short of monster holes and class V whitewater. Most midsize rafts cost between $800 and $6,000 for the bare boat. New rafts that cost less than this will be of pretty marginal quality over the long term. Hunting down a good used one is always a sensible option, especially if you're not in a hurry, for good used rafts are seldom easily available.

In addition to the bare raft, you'll need a rowing frame (at $500 to $1,500), oars (around $150 each), seats, a pump, patch kit, a strong frame-fitting cooler (another $60 or more), and ropes. An anchor system is a good idea, too. Custom-made front and rear knee braces and an anchor system for the ultimate fly-fishing raft cost $500 or more. Anchors go for around $75 and up.

On the plus side for rafts is their ability to be rolled up and transported in a vehicle without the added cost of a trailer, as well as the fact that they take up less storage space. Some frequent river runners do keep and transport rafts on trailers because it eliminates setup and take-down time on stream.

Rafts have that built-in buoyancy that makes them a safer, more forgiving craft in demanding water situations. They also draw less water when floating and are the best choice for some smaller shallow rivers, especially during late summer's low flows. I use rafts on some shallow rivers and drift boats on others, depending on water depth and launch-site quality. In many places, accesses have no actual ramp and boats have to be carried, sometimes down hills and over fences.

Rafts don't row quite as well as hard-hull boats. Nor are they as comfortable to stand up in and cast from. There are, however, modifications that can improve these deficits to some degree. Self-bailing rafts, which have inflated floors, row better than traditional models, while allowing any water shipped from waves, rain, or dripping waders to drain. Knee braces can be custom-built to make standing to fish easier in rafts. Wooden floors can also be added to firm up the footing.

Raft design and materials bear consideration, too. White-water rafts tend to have larger-diameter tubes to increase buoyancy and fend off big waves. Upturning of the front and back ends is more pronounced for the same reason. These qualities don't hurt in a fishing boat except under one condition—wind. If you plan to fish where waters are mellow and wind can be high (much of Montana, for instance), a lower-profile raft might be a better choice.

The high bow upturn makes some rafts more comfortable to stand up in and lean against at the front of the boat, and it works to some degree as a knee brace. Lower-profile rafts don't

Self-bailing rafts have inflated floors with portholes around the floor connection that let water run out. These float shallower water than conventional rafts or drift boats.

Catamaran rafts come in one-man, two- or three-man, and on up to 30-foot giants used to float the Grand Canyon. They're a little cheaper than rafts for their size and can be ideal choices for many anglers. MARK LISK PHOTO COURTESY OF OUTCAST SPORTING GEAR

have the same built-in knee-brace qualities, but they don't catch as much wind, either. These benefit most from the addition of fabricated knee braces, which can be built on an extended rowing frame. Most design features carry performance tradeoffs to some degree.

Catamaran rafts are another option. In the smallest sizes, they have come to replace float tubes as high-performance one-person fishing craft. Most use oars and swim fins for a dual-option maneuvering: oars for major ferries, fins for slowing and minor positioning while fishing. Anchor systems are usually included. You'll even see electric trolling motors on some.

Larger catamaran rafts of 12 to 18 feet (and on up to monsters used to run the Grand Canyon) are available and somewhat popular in whitewater circles. These weigh less, row well, obviously don't ship water, and fold up into relatively small packages. The rowing frame is by nature rather complex and thus pricey. It can have desired features built into it, including full-length floor, bow and stern knee braces, and an anchor system. Many rowing-frame builders do custom jobs. The end product costs about 25 percent less than a fully rigged regular-quality raft and can be a viable option.

High-quality rafts are made from two basic material families: Hypalon/neoprene and PVC, an advanced reinforced vinyl. The former was common in rafts for years. The higher the percentage of Hypalon in the laminate, the longer-lived and better-made the raft tends to be. Avon rafts have always been leaders in the material quality and river boat fields, though many other manufacturers build high-quality products, some of which are better designed for certain uses and cost less than Avons.

The other material that's come into prominence in the last decade is reinforced PVC laminate. Improvements in materials, bonding, and design have helped boats made of this material get a big market share of late. These aren't the flimsy vinyl boats you may be thinking of; they're priced right up there with Hypalon rafts, though some are significantly cheaper. One feature of PVC boats is their greater rigidity when inflated. This translates into a raft that rows more like a hard-hull boat while keeping its shape in severe turbulence. PVC boats don't buckle as much as Hypalon boats do in big holes. Whitewater floaters like the improved handling characteristics of a stiff PVC boat. Anglers can take advantage of that rowing benefit, too. The self-bailing models row particularly well. Raft materials, concepts, and designs will continue to evolve.

All in all, rafts are the best choice for many float fishers, depending on frequency and location of use, stream depth,

COMPARING FISHING CRAFT DESIGNS

RAFTS

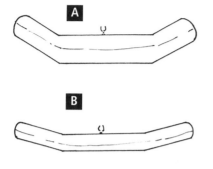

Rafts built for serious whitewater have larger-diameter tubes and greater upturn (rocker) fore and aft to better handle big water. They also catch more wind.

If mellower rivers twisting through breeze-frequented terrain are in your forecast, consider rafts with smaller tube diameters and less upturn. Self-bailing rafts will skim over shallower riffles more easily than conventional rafts.

There are plenty of raft makes and models to choose from. Consider your local water, wind, and fishing conditions before choosing.

potential whitewater use, ramp availability, and camp-cargo hauling capabilities. They save the cost of a trailer and can be stored in a small area (out of the sun's harmful rays). They're forgiving in demanding water, can bounce off obstacles, and are more likely to make it through misguided rowing adventures than other craft are. A raft package can be bought for a bit less than a pram or drift boat; consequently, rafts remain the most popular floating choice in the West.

Prams

Modern rowing prams are something of a cross between full-size drift boats (with their pronounced rocker, or bottom curvature) and flat-bottomed johnboats. Most are a little shorter than drift boats, with somewhat lower sides, especially in the front end. Some are a lot like a drift boat, with 2 feet cut off the nose. Their square-ended look is perhaps less aesthetically pleasing than that of a drift boat but better fits the rowing requirements

DRIFT BOATS

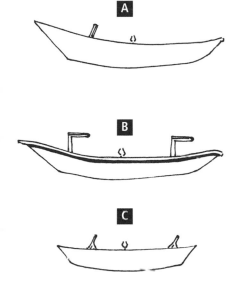

A Traditional drift boats were built with serious whitewater in mind on the rough-and-tumble steelhead rivers of the West Coast. They're stable and comfortable to fish from but catch a lot of wind and are easier for trout to see on flat water.

B Lower-profile drift boats can be better choices for many easy-flowing trout rivers where the wind has been known to blow. They're easier to get in and out of, too.

C A variety of rowing prams make excellent choices as well. They handle moderate water, weigh and cost less, and have a low wind profile. Some lack knee braces, though, and are not as easy or comfortable to stand up in and cast from.

Drift boats come in a variety of designs, too. Smaller rowing prams add to your hard-hull choices.

of many waters. Most have a modified rocker and maneuver very well because of a lowered wind profile. This alone can be important.

The lighter weight, efficient use of space, slightly smaller size, low wind profile, and excellent handling properties have made prams a popular choice among today's recreational anglers and guides. Although they are not cheap by any means, they are less expensive than full-size 16- to 17-foot drift boats. Some one- to two-person prams have even been designed to fit in the bed of a standard pickup truck and are just lightweight enough to lift onto one. Prams range in size from these smaller, 8- to 10-foot craft on up to 16 feet. The smallest ones seem most

A FULLY RIGGED FISHING RAFT

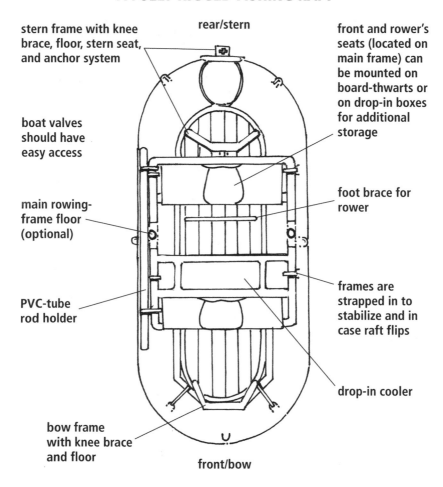

stern frame with knee brace, floor, stern seat, and anchor system

rear/stern

front and rower's seats (located on main frame) can be mounted on board-thwarts or on drop-in boxes for additional storage

boat valves should have easy access

main rowing-frame floor (optional)

foot brace for rower

PVC-tube rod holder

frames are strapped in to stabilize and in case raft flips

drop-in cooler

bow frame with knee brace and floor

front/bow

popular on mellower stretches of West Coast salmon rivers, where big-fish fever makes river addicts out of many. Fourteen-foot models are quite popular on Rocky Mountain trout rivers, and the larger models add more storage capacity and overnighting potential. Though some small to midsize prams could be car topped, most are trailered for ease of use.

Rowing prams are priced lower than full-size drift boats and have a reduced wind profile and the ability to sneak up closer to spooky trout.

Float fishers who ply rivers with little or no real whitewater could find rowing prams to be an ideal choice. The only downside to some of them is that they lack the knee braces found in most drift boats, which make standing to cast a pleasure. It is easy to fall out of a pram if one is standing unsupported. However, inventive owners can add braces in both bow and stern. Many homemade stern knee braces also incorporate a backrest for the rower's seat, which otherwise is not usually found. This adds some back comfort for boatmen spending long days on the river. The latest generations of prams do incorporate knee braces, rod holders, and improved storage. Constant improvements are seen today.

Because most prams are a little smaller than full-size drift boats, they have a little less storage space. Most are well designed, though, and adequate for day use. Anchor systems and trailers are generally included in the purchase package.

In big water or heavy rapids, a raft or drift boat would be a safer choice, but a rowing pram's handling characteristics allow it to be navigated through challenging stretches quite well. Ultimately, a pram would be a little easier to capsize, especially in the hands of a novice rower. On mellower trout rivers, though, today's prams command a large share of the float-fishing market.

One other benefit of lower-sided prams is their reduced visibility to fish. They're also easy to get in and out of when wadefishing in waders. High-sided drift boats with standing anglers spook fish sooner where waters are flat and fishing pressure is high. Trout can see them from farther away, so drift-boat anglers sometimes have to cast farther to overcome this handicap. Prams with seated anglers allow a closer approach to fish. Dull earth-tone hull colors are better choices than bright white or brilliant colors. With the growing fishing pressure on most rivers these days, every advantage helps. Staying low and out of sight isn't a bad place to start.

Kick boats and pontoon craft offer great fishing potential at a reasonable price. Don't pump up and assemble your craft on the ramp, blocking traffic. Do it off to the side and carry it in when you're done.

Personal Watercraft

From float tubes, kick boats, pontoon craft, and on up to kayaks, one-man canoes, and mini-prams, a whole industry has developed around affordable watercraft. They can be found in your local fishing shop, Cabela's and fly-fishing catalogs, and on websites near and far. You can nickel-and-dime your way from a couple of hundred to a couple of thousand dollars or more. For ease of transport and rampless put-ins, they can't be beat.

First to hit the scene were float tubes. These are fine for lakes and slow rivers. Obviously, they're not designed for speed or distance and are dangerous in demanding navigation situations. Nonetheless, it's affordable river transport if you know your water and your limitations.

Better than float tubes are pontoon craft, especially for rivers that require a lot of maneuvering or distant crossings. With pontoon boats, you have a hull rocker and length, and footrests to keep your body completely out of the water. Now your hull works as it should. You use oars for major maneuvers, just like any other rowing craft, and fins for slowing while fishing. Should a hazard or other angler come up, you can get the heck out of the way. Pontoon boats generally have anchor systems, storage options, and even room for a cooler. Some have knee braces for standing and casting, stripping baskets, and rod holders. A few are even rigged for small or electric motors! One thing to consider with pontoon boats is their length and quality. Typically, they run from 6 to 10 feet. The longer they are, the more weight they'll properly support, and the faster they'll be across the water. Quality construction, added length, and features all add up to more expense. Good ones cost from $500 to more than $1,500.

If I were going to fish alone all the time, I would add another feature, a second anchor system. (Actually, I would add this to any craft.) On this system, I would run a rope with a length of chain on it. Dragging chain slows down your boat, keeps it in line, and reduces side-wind blow. It's the same effect as constantly kicking with fins, but without constantly kicking with fins! On slower rivers, just a foot or two of chain, dragging lengthwise, is all you need. Deeper, faster water requires heavier or longer chain, and a bit more rope. You do have to watch for snaggy bottoms, like downed trees and angular boulders. Keep a knife handy to quickly cut an anchor or chain rope that gets irretrievably stuck; on very swift water, snagging an anchor or chain can yank your boat under water. Chain dragged lengthwise isn't all that snaggy, though.

The small johnboat is still a practical one- or two-person craft. They're cheap, and dozens of used ones are always for sale. Its weak point is a crappy rowing and oarlock setup. To vastly improve it, so you can use longer oars, the oarlocks need to be enhanced. Ideally, you want to move a reinforced oarlock

ENHANCING OARLOCKS

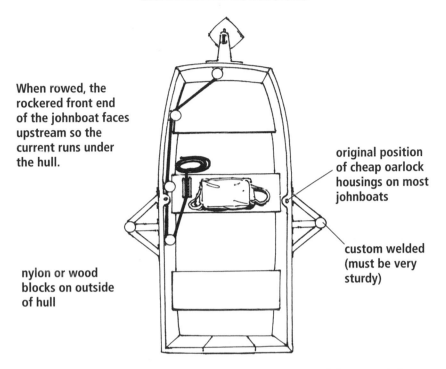

When rowed, the rockered front end of the johnboat faces upstream so the current runs under the hull.

original position of cheap oarlock housings on most johnboats

custom welded (must be very sturdy)

nylon or wood blocks on outside of hull

By custom-building an outrigged oarlock (extended beyond the gunwale by a few inches to a foot), longer, higher-quality oars can be used. Much more power and control can be exerted. You can use the crawl stroke too.

The seat and oarlock relationship may have to be adjusted for optimal performance. A quality rowing seat and bow-mount anchor system are welcome additions. These can benefit other small craft as well. Use coolers and gear for ballast to level the boat.

housing outside the hull a bit, by a few inches to a foot. (Ever see a racing scull's rigging?) This allows longer oars for better leverage and enables you to do the crawl stroke, too, which you otherwise can't.

By the way, you point the curved (rockered) front end of a johnboat upstream to row and maneuver, so the water runs under and lifts it. Don't row with the square motor-mount end pointed upstream; it just plows a lot of water. A bow-mounted anchor system and comfortable rowing seat are decided pluses.

A small johnboat thus rigged (perhaps with truck bed liner sprayed in to dull the sound and stop rivet leaks) is a pretty serviceable craft for mellower rivers. A double front-ended model johnboat, with no square stern or motor mount, would have rocker like a more expensive pram. Add a real oarlock arrangement, and a 52- to 55-inch-wide floor, and that manufacturer would have a bigger market share.

Drift Boats

The generic name "drift boat," apparently adopted for lack of a better term, usually designates river dories of various designs. Some people call any river dory a McKenzie boat. This, too, is imprecise, because the McKenzie boat is a localized design common to the Oregon river of the same name. It's quite different in form from most other dories.

The dory is an ancient design that is widely used in seas and oceans around the world. Its adaptation to river use (with an increased rocker for maneuvering) came in the late 1800s on coastal Oregon rivers, where whitewater and big fish coincide. Over the course of the century, they became an accepted craft on swift trout, salmon, and steelhead rivers across the West. They're now seen back East, in New Zealand, and on other rivers worldwide.

Several manufacturers build dories of fiberglass, aluminum, and wood. Each material offers some advantage. Drift boats of 14 to 17 feet are most commonly constructed, with 15- to 16-foot models being most popular. (Dories are traditionally measured along the gunwales and not down the center. A 16-foot board, for instance, was bent to shape the sides of a boat; thus

KEEPING AN ANCHORED BOAT
FROM SWINGING IN THE CURRENT

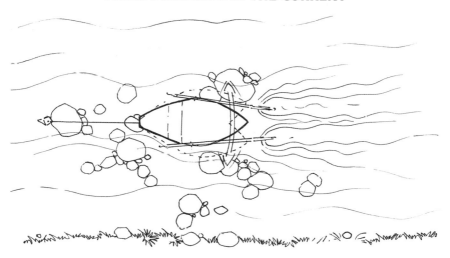

Anchored boats tend to swing in the current due to the curved, or rockered, bottom. Wakes created by boat swing can spook fish.

If a rower holds the oars with the blades perpendicular to the surface and parallel to the boat's length, swinging will largely cease. They act as downstream rudders. (Boat swing also drags the anchor and interferes with fly drifts.) A mechanism to lock the oar down tight to the boat in this position would be one of the best possible improvements for drift boats. The rower would then be free to do other things rather than holding the oars in that position for hours a day.

the boat was a 16-footer. The center line itself would be closer to 15 feet.) Its stability, maneuverability, fishing comfort, and style make the drift boat a welcome addition to many a river angler's arsenal, and next to the vehicle he uses to pull it, the most expensive.

On the plus side, drift boats can handle rough water, offer stand-up fishing comfort with their knee braces, and have ample storage space and excellent rowing qualities. They have a rocker for maneuvering in fast water, respond well to the crawl stroke, and can be rowed to a standstill in a good current. Most come with anchor systems, seats with backrests, protective rod tubes, and other options with anglers in mind. Rear knee braces are standard, too, which is good, because it's the stern angler who sometimes falls out of the boat. Winter steelheaders even put propane heaters in drift boats. The best ones have graceful lines, snag-free finishes, and a stylish look. Prices now range from $7,500 to $10,000, including trailer. Build-it-yourself woodboat kits with precut parts can be bought for around $2,500.

But drift boats have some negatives. They generally require a reasonable ramp from which to launch and take out (though it's easier to slide one down a bank than it is to pull it back up). Most weigh close to 300 pounds, a little much to bust brush with. Many rivers have adequate ramps, so this won't be a problem in most locales. Exploratory types who shun crowds might want to stick with rafts or other light craft that make nonramp put-ins much easier.

Drift boats are a little hard to get in and out of, especially for the less agile, although today's low-sided models are a great improvement. If a party stops often to get out and wade-fish, this could present a problem for some anglers wearing waders. In this situation, a raft or pram would be easier to get in and out of. I've often wondered why manufacturers don't build a watertight door in the front end of drift boats because this area is above the waterline. This would be easy to do and would certainly make getting in and out of a high-sided boat easier, especially in midstream at wadable gravel bars.

On small, shallow rivers, drift boats can draw too much water for easy navigation. A drift boat with three people and gear draws 8 to 12 inches of water. A raft or johnboat with a similar load draws only half that. You can beat, dent, and chip the heck out of a drift boat's hull during a day's drift on a too-shallow river. A pram is better in shallow water, and a raft is better yet.

Although drift boats are usually the most expensive river rowing craft (some rafts and prams are right up there in price, too), they usually last a long time and have good resale value if maintained. Used drift boats in my area are snapped up quickly because so few seem to be available at any one time.

Last but certainly not least on the negative side is the drift boat's great ability to catch wind. It will sail like a leaf in middling blows and become difficult to control in your every-third-day, east-slope-of-the-Rockies chinook gale. Forty- to sixty-mile-per-hour gusts keep experienced boatmen on their toes and get novices into blister- and callus-building high gear. Getting blown into banks or navigational hazards is a distinct possibility for beginners in drift boats. Some manufacturers and designs are

I like my low-pro Hyde for its superior hull design, low wind profile, and interior layout. I especially like the elevated rower's floor, which keeps excess water from sloshing around my feet.

better or worse than others. There are extra-high-sided ones built with whitewater in mind (which are not so good in the wind), and low-sided ones now being targeted at mellower but windy trout rivers. Those fishing more sheltered river valleys with some whitewater prefer the high-sided models.

Here in Montana's big wind country ("big sky" is just a cover-up), low-sided models are often preferred. High-sided drift boats with rolled gunwales are the worst for wind, in my experience. This is a construction feature of some fiberglass boats that stiffens the sides and eases the task of manufacture but catches additional wind. Bear these factors in mind when it's time to choose a boat.

DRIFT BOAT AND PRAM CONSTRUCTION OPTIONS
Three basic materials are used to build river rowing craft: aluminum, fiberglass laminates, and wood. Each material has its devotees and detractors. Aluminum and fiberglass are chosen most perhaps for their low maintenance requirements, but there are some other reasons.

Aluminum
Aluminum drift boats are favored by many, especially by steelhead and salmon fishermen of the Northwest, for their durability. Where rock-slamming whitewater and big waves are daily occurrences, aluminum seems to be the material of choice. Good aluminum boats aren't cheap but should give a lifetime of service, disasters aside. Wrapped drift boats can be straightened and welded back into serviceable condition, something that's not as likely to happen with glass and wood boats.

Negative qualities of aluminum boats include noise. Water lapping against the hull makes a faint ringing sound, and anything dropped in the boat can alarm fish by the transmitted sound. This minor irritant can be overcome with the installation of some outdoor carpet or spray-in bed liner on the floor and a little way up the insides.

Aluminum sticks to rocks more than glass or wood, should the boat be high-centered. Rocks, especially coarse or jagged rocks, bite into the aluminum a bit, bringing the boat to a halt on top of a barely submerged midstream rock. In some cases, the water around such a rock will be so deep that you can't get out of the boat to push it off. A combination of rocking, oar levering, spinning, and hard rowing is then needed to break free. There are synthetic skid plates and paint-on hull treatments such as Gluvit that alleviate this problem. Though they are quite pricey per gallon, many aluminum-boat owners use these treatments to coat their hulls.

Another complaint one hears about aluminum is its easy transmission of temperature. Cold water can chill the aluminum in which you're spending your day. Modern insulated clothing minimizes this annoyance. Winter steelheaders carry small portable propane heaters for angling comfort.

Uncoated aluminum can leave a grayish residue on hands and clothes. This, too, is a small point, because the seats are usually made of a different material. Many aluminum boats come painted, or at least have coated gunwales and knee braces.

Most problems aside, aluminum remains a good choice for prams and drift boats, especially where hull abuse can be expected.

Fiberglass

This maintenance-free material is popular because of its ease of manufacture, moldability, longevity, and moderate price. Although there are expensive, tricked-out fiberglass drift boats on the market, the basic models are the lowest-priced new drift boats to be found.

Even though fiberglass is maintenance-free, it will ultimately last longer and look better if it is kept out of the sun when not in use. Sunshine is the enemy of synthetics and most exterior finishes. A boat cover is desirable, a garage better yet. Although sun damage to the actual laminate would take decades to appear, color fading of the exterior gel coat and interior paint will be noticeable much sooner.

Fiberglass slides over rocks with greater ease than other materials. Some models are designed to allow the floor to flex, further facilitating this sliding, nontipping benefit. Too much rock hopping and floor flexing will begin to deteriorate the laminate's rigidity, though. It's not something you want to take to extremes.

Although fiberglass can puncture and chip and is more likely to break up in serious collisions and wraps, most glass boats are built so heavily in the hull as to make daily wear and tear inappreciable, even over a long period of time. Fiberglass is also the easiest boat material to repair. A boat can even be quickly patched riverside, should the owner have the foresight to carry a fiberglass patch kit. The same patch kit can repair a wood boat, too. Duct tape even works for small jobs as a quick fix.

Some fiberglass drift boats are the ugly ducklings of the riverboat world. Although they are utilitarian enough, it's hard to ignore their tubby, homely look. Others are graceful and pleasing to the eye, though the splatter paint used on the interior of most fiberglass boats never has turned me on. Its purpose of hiding both dirt and manufacturer's flaws and rough edges just gives a cheap look to the finished product, to my mind.

Some high-sided, rolled-gunwale fiberglass boats seem to be worst of all in wind. The rolled gunwale catches a little more wind than a straight one does, making a boat lurch over in strong side winds. A leaning boat is hard to row because the oar tends to hit your low-side knee. Whether made so by wind or leaning humans, a heeled-over drift boat is difficult or impossible to row. And although no river boat is much fun in the wind, some are certainly worse than others. Rolled gun-

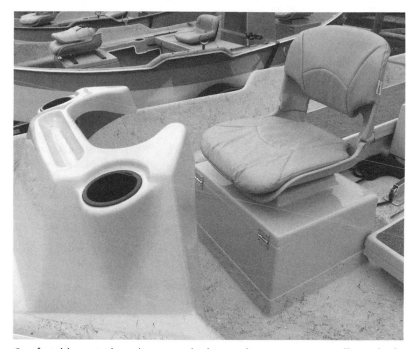

Comfortable seats, knee braces, rod tubes, and gear storage are all standard on most of today's drift boats. Check various models for the features that best suit your budget and fishing.

wales could be cut off some old high-sided models by the industrious and replaced with wood (steamed ash is best). This should improve wind resistance a little and improve its looks a lot.

Fiberglass boats have few other downsides, although they are not ultimately as repairable as aluminum after a major wrap. What remain are usually design weaknesses rather than material flaws. Check the market for hull designs, seat and storage options, front and rear knee braces, anchor systems, rod holders, color options, and the like. With the perfection of low-profile fiberglass boats, I've added a Hyde to my arsenal.

ROWING A LEANING BOAT

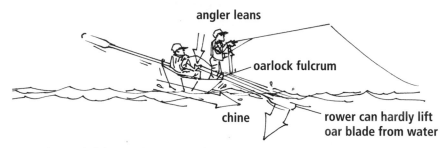

angler leans

oarlock fulcrum

chine

rower can hardly lift
oar blade from water

When a drift boat is leaning too far to one side (usually because the bow angler is leaning too far to one side and not keeping centered), the rower can hardly pick the oar blade up out of the water, for the oar handle now hits his knee. And because the hull is no longer flat on the water, the chine now acts as a curved centerboard, disrupting the boat's forward drift. These two elements combined make a leaning drift boat or pram very difficult to row. Wind and whitewater sometimes produce the same oar handle and knee conflict. In some boats this situation can be improved if the oarlock position is slightly raised. Keep anglers centered.

Good boats have adjustable seat positions so that the boat will trim out properly, whether two or three people are in the craft. A drift boat that plows water with the stern when someone's sitting aft is harder to row. This is a design flaw that some manufacturers seem to have no interest in correcting. It originated in the old West Coast salmon-fishing days, when boats had two anglers in the front and none in the stern. Putting an angler in the stern made them plow water. Water should not hit the stern; it should slide under it and hit only the bottom, even with an angler seated in the back. Many boats have their sterns lifted free of the water when an angler in the back of the boat stands up to fish and leans into a rear knee brace. This is how most boats with two casters and a boatman row best, if the anglers are secure in knee braces and not falling around the boat.

Wood

There are certainly many devotees of good wooden river boats. "Hey, nice-looking boat," is something you don't hear much when rowing fiberglass or aluminum. The beauty of clear finished wood on water is undeniable. And it doesn't need as much maintenance as some people think if it's built right in the first place and kept out of the elements when not in use. The sun is the enemy of a wooden boat's finish.

What makes wood a realistic option, even for low-maintenance devotees, is epoxy saturation. A boat that's well built from the right types of wood (those that water doesn't hurt, like ash, spruce, cedar, and quality marine ply) and that's coated, sealed, or fiberglassed with epoxy will last a long time without much refinishing. A recreational weekend floater who keeps his boat fully covered or garaged should be able to go several years between cosmetic Varathane applications over the epoxy base. Heavily used parts like gunwales, knee braces, and seats might need a coat of Varathane or other hard exterior sun-resistant finish once a season. Any punctures or serious abrasions should be treated immediately, of course, to preserve the wood. Nylon skid plates are a worthwhile option for the bottom of wooden boats plied on more abrasive rivers.

Most of the minor damage to my 18-year-old cedar drift boat came from the few times I lent it out. (If someone asks to borrow it now, I just walk away laughing.) Rowers of good wooden boats are more likely to avoid rocks than other floaters are, which only goes toward truly mastering rowing skills.

Wooden boats are less likely candidates for serious rock-slamming rivers, for obvious reasons. Although a wooden boat can be built structurally to take it, one should expect more frequent refinishing and repair jobs. Many of Montana's trout rivers are gravel- and cobble-bottomed. A skilled rower rarely has to hit anything; my boat is 18 years old now and has almost no real bottom wear. The chines, where bottom and sides meet, take the most abuse. I've reinforced mine twice over the years with the simple addition of a layer of fiberglass tape and epoxy.

Some wooden one- to two-person prams fit in the beds of pickups and are light enough to lift. "Cedar strip" and cross-laminated cedar-veneer boats are particularly light and epoxy-sealed. They can weigh half as much as plywood, fiberglass, or aluminum boats. Using the latest wood-construction technology, one could even build a 16-foot drift boat that weighs in at just over 100 pounds. If your rivers are easy on boats and ramps are scarce, a 60- to 200-pound pram or drift boat is much easier to muscle around than a 300-pound fiberglass one.

There is a latent pleasure in building and maintaining your own wooden craft. When you've sanded and finished every beautiful grain and seen it reflect across the water in every light, it deepens the river experience that much more. Just like tying your own flies, building your own boat takes you deeper into the river world.

Wooden boats are not for everybody, but the technology is there to allow you to buy or build low-maintenance and beautiful wooden craft. I, for one, hate to see the whole world go plastic. Wood boats row well, have a great feel in the water, and can have extremely long lives when maintained. They are by nature expensive when new (and sometimes dirt cheap when old and neglected), but your hours on the water seem more pleasurable on wood. Wooden boat kits can be bought for around $2,500.

RIGGING THE CRAFT

Properly outfitting a boat enhances its fishability and comfort. Neat arrangements that don't tangle fly lines and have plenty of storage for gear and food are desirable. Anchor systems are a great asset, along with comfortable seating and knee braces. A well-rigged craft makes for a pleasurable day astream.

Rafts

Rafts are often sold with no accessories other than a pump and patch kit. Rowing frames, oars, oarlocks, and seats are extra. Boat dealers often offer raft and frame packages. It's a good idea to look at a number of them and scan the catalogs to see what's available before buying. You'd hate to buy one rowing frame (at $400 to $1,500) and then see one you like much better.

Rowing frames are your biggest consideration and expense after the raft itself. They vary in size, weight, materials, and design. Some have floors, which are good for storing gear and protecting the floor of your raft; some don't. Floors add more weight, so if weight is a major consideration (as when flying, horsepacking, or carrying equipment into a wilderness or rampless river), aluminum floorless frames are a wise choice. I've seen relatively lightweight homemade frames made of PVC plumbing pipe. Frames may be made from bent and welded conduit. Heavy homemade wooden ones are old standbys but are now waning in popularity as the prefab market becomes more diverse. Whether homemade, catalog-chosen, or custom-built, it pays to consider how a rowing frame can best serve your needs.

Rowing frames serve several purposes. First and foremost, they stiffen the raft and provide a solid base from which to row. Be aware that the little rubber oarlocks that come glued to the tubes of some cheaper rafts aren't very good performers in demanding rowing situations. Frames provide seating structure for the rower and bow angler. Frames also hold coolers for food and drink. Some are designed to house drop-in storage boxes for gear. These may be included with frame and, of course, add to its cost. One handy arrangement is to have drop-in boxes (which can be carried up to a camp or into your house for loading) with seats on top. Anytime you have gear serving double duty, you come out ahead. Frames provide storage decks for things that would otherwise fall off the raft's round tubes, ending up wet on the floor or in the river. Frames with built-in solid floors add storage capability and comfort for standing while protecting the raft floor from puncture and abrasion.

There should be no weight on the raft floor itself; it must be able to stretch up and over rocks. Any weight sitting on the raft floor acts like an anvil or cutting board: The raft floor is cut or punctured between the weight on top of it and the river rocks underneath. That is why rowing-frame floors are important. A full-length floor can be built, though it will become rather heavy. Weight might be less of a consideration for some than optimal storage capabilities. One could even sleep on a full-length floor and design a tent that sets up on the raft frame. This would eliminate the need to set camp for one- or two-person trips.

The ultimate raft setup would include an anchor system and rear knee braces. These aren't always available and might have to be custom-made. The whole raft and frame industry has historically been more concerned with whitewater than with fishing, but this has changed.

Different types of seats can be attached to a raft frame. Folding, padded, sturdy models are best for use and transport. Some are built on pedestals to give casters a little extra height (which makes the rower feel safer).

Traditionally, raft frames didn't have anchor systems or knee braces. Anglers added them themselves or had them custom-made. You may still have to do this today, though more are available. Two- or even three-part frames are seen: the main center frame in its traditional form, a stern frame with seat and anchor system, and a front piece for a knee brace. A rear knee brace could be built on either the main or rear frame. A full-length frame incorporating all these features can be built if transport and storage aren't a problem. Breakdown frames are made, too. They break down into several pieces for transport but always seem a bit of a pain to put back together. Stern

Cargo nets and big folding tables are used to pile camping gear on. Don't load gear directly on the raft floor because that can puncture it when you hit rocks. Some fishing groups will take one raft just for camp gear in addition to fishing boats.

frames are even made to house motors and gas tanks, but rafts need to be stiffened for motorization. Even then they can only handle smaller engines. Rafts like Zodiacs, specifically designed to use a motor, have strong built-in transoms and can be used for rowing rivers. They are a good choice if both lake and river fishing are in your future.

Other accessories for rafts can be used when an angler is not in the stern. Cargo decks made of webbing and nets to tie down gear are popular. A big folding table can be lashed to the back of the boat for camping, and gear can be piled on top of it (see the illustration in Chapter 7). You could make a cargo rain cover, although most floaters use a folded camp tarp under the netting to do the job. These are tied down to D rings that come built into the raft and the rowing frame. Cargo decks are useful for camping trips and, on smaller rafts, for day trips with only one angler. I have a 10-foot raft I use for two-person trips that can be transported in a compact car. With the rising price of gas, this can become an issue for some. It's a lot cheaper to Honda the raft than to pull the drift boat with my pickup! Such boats are light enough for one person to carry.

One last desirable accessory is a rod holder. Many floaters tie a 9-foot length of PVC pipe along the outside of their rafts, using the D rings as tie downs. Extra rods can be safely stored this way. Be sure to add some securing device, because I have seen rods work their way out of such tubes over time and slide out into the river. It is handy to have a second rod rigged with an alternative fly, though. The less clutter around the boat (such as a bunch of rod cases), the fewer tangles you'll have to fool with throughout the day.

Prams

Most prams are smaller than full-size drift boats and economize somewhat on storage and knee braces. Most have three seats and an anchor system. Smaller models may have only two seats. There are even one-person models around, popular on mellower West Coast salmon rivers.

Some prams don't come with knee braces, but adding homemade ones isn't too difficult for the do-it-yourselfer. Some type of sturdy wood setup is easy enough to figure out and attach. Otherwise, hunt the market for models that do have them. The latest prams from Hyde and other fiberglass manufacturers include knee braces these days, and rod tubes, too.

Additional storage can be added to some models by affixing removable waterproof boxes under the thwarts (seat supports), except where pedestal seat mounts are used. A rod holder of some sort is always a good idea.

Most prams and drift boats have anchor systems. These feed the rope up to the rower's position via pulleys or a floor-

ANCHOR DESIGNS

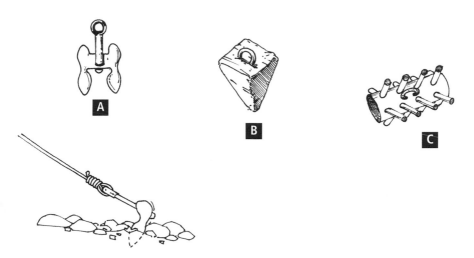

Different anchors can be chosen to meet regional demands.

A. A digging-type anchor is used only where finer cobble, gravel, and silts make up the bottom structure. It will snag in rocks. You can use a lighter-weight anchor, though, because the digging bite enhances its hold.

B. The inverted pyramid is a common and good all-around anchor. Thirty pounds is a typical weight for a full-size drift boat.

C. The studded cylinder is used on rounded-boulder rivers like Montana's Madison. It may even need to be overweighted, say 35–40 pounds.

mounted tube. They have either a jam cleat or a more sophisticated self-locking foot-release mechanism within easy reach so the rower can control everything. Some anchor systems feed the rope up the side, others down the floor at the centerline. Most boaters seem to prefer the floor mounted, foot-release, automatic rope-locking models these days. The anchor can be released while the craft is being rowed, allowing the boatman to perfectly position the boat for anchoring in range of rising fish. When the anchor is pulled in, the rower just lets go of the rope as it automatically jams. He doesn't have to manually jam the rope in a cleat. The only negative is that the rope piled on the floor can tangle around your feet and on its way out. In freezing weather, ice may inhibit the rope from passing through the narrow tube that feeds it to the stern pulleys. I have the older-system side-led rope and jam cleat. It serves me well— rowers tend to adapt to the equipment at hand. By the way, the anchor is lowered, not dropped. It can splash a seated stern angler, and anchors thudding on the bottom can spook fish. Once it has entered the water, it can then be fully lowered.

Anchors vary in weight and design to meet the demands of different bottom types. The most common design is probably the inverted pyramid, and average weight is 30 pounds. The inverted pyramid bites into bottom strata well enough and isn't too likely to get snagged. Sand and fine gravel bottoms allow digging-type designs, which can be lighter in weight. Some of these look like miniature ship anchors; others are thinner and more streamlined. Avoid the cheap plastic-coated ones found in many department stores. The plastic coating doesn't allow the anchor to pivot on its stem as it should, thus negating its bottom-digging abilities. On swift, bouldery rivers like Montana's Madison, some heavier-duty anchors may be seen. One design features a heavy horizontal cylinder with big metal studs sticking out in all directions. It would make a London punk rocker feel right at home on the boat! This anchor grabs the rounded stones well without snagging. There are, of course, other designs around, including such homemade mainstays as sections of railroad track and large coffee cans filled with cement or lead with an eyebolt molded in. Any big hunk of scrap metal or chain can work wherever snagging isn't a problem. Anchors don't always hold where you first drop them. Tailwinds and fast or deep water will cause them to drag a bit. Anticipate this, slow down, and drop it in advance.

The double rope hanging from this anchor system indicates that an underwater pulley is being used. It attaches to the anchor and reduces the pull-up effort by half. Since anchors weigh 30 pounds, this saves a lot of labor over the course of the day.

The anchor rope should be of high quality, soft and thick enough to be comfortable on your hands and not tangle as it goes through the pulleys. Avoid harsh-textured rope, especially the cheap yellow polypropylene stuff seen in most department stores. It stretches, has memory, and gets coils and kinks in it. It's rough on the hands, too. Tight, sophisticated weaves of polypropylene are best. They're memory-free, easy on the hands, and don't stretch. They cost a little more per foot but are well worth it, as you'll discover after lifting and dropping the anchor hundreds of times. About 25 to 35 feet of rope should do. Tie a knot in your end so it can't accidentally run out through the pulleys and be lost. It should be as thick as possible yet still glide freely through the pulleys and floor tube. The only minor downside to these tight-weave ropes is that it can be very difficult to unsnag a barbed fly from them. Believe me, a few will be left in place there!

Most boaters affix a quick-release attachment of some kind to the anchor end of the rope. Many prefer to remove the anchor for transport. Others just pull some rope out and lay the anchor in the boat, which is not a good idea unless it is in a protective container. It can bounce around there just enough to do a little cosmetic damage, heavy though it is. Some boaters just let it dangle from the anchor system during transportation, which is not good. It's not too unusual to see a rig take off down the road dragging the anchor on a length of rope behind the trailer. The boater is last seen heading into the sunset with the anchor swinging wildly from side to side. Anchor holders are available on some boat trailers and on boats themselves. These are a good idea and can be added on.

Boaters sometimes forget to rope in the anchor after landing and trailering their craft. This is more common than you might imagine, so be sure to stow your anchor before leaving. I had a bad habit of losing an anchor every year or so by leaving it at the take-out. I'd unhook it from the rope, lay it on the ground while packing up, and forget to pick it up, because the dull gray color can be difficult to spot on a ramp at twilight. Always double-check the ground around the ramp area, and the top of your vehicle (where anglers sometimes put rods), for possessions, making sure you've left nothing behind at the put-in and take-out.

Occasionally, a boat will come off a trailer during transportation, not having been securely fastened. This can cause extensive hull damage. A vehicle or two end up submerged in the river, too, usually due to faulty parking brakes on a steep ramp. This is a real shocker to the owner! I lost a truck once on a January duck hunt, before a winter's dawn brightened the sky. The river had flooded earlier in the winter and receded. The ramp was solid ice but covered with enough dirt and debris that I couldn't tell it was ice in the darkness. While we were unloading the boat, the truck started sliding out into the river and sank out of sight. Not a good start.

Pay attention to all aspects of loading and unloading. That is where most equipment is lost. Having your name, address, and phone number on every single piece of equipment will help you regain some lost gear.

Drift Boats

There are enough makes of drift boats on the market these days to fit most desires. Get all the brochures, look at as many as you can, try rowing some demos when possible, and find the features you want. Most come complete with seats, storage, front knee brace (rear ones may come as standard or optional equipment), anchor system, rod tubes, and trailer. They may or may not include oars (different people like different oar types) and a cover. These often cost extra. Oars cost around $200 each. Fitted boat covers go for $350 to $600.

Few modifications should be necessary to a well-appointed drift boat. There are some that might be necessary, however, on certain makes and on some older used models. Sometimes the oarlock position is too low. The oar handles will occasionally hit the rower's knees when he is rowing, particularly if an angler is leaning to one side or the other and isn't staying to center. This dilemma makes rowing difficult, but a surprising number of boats I've rowed have this fault. In this case, the oarlock housing, usually wood or hard nylon blocks, can be rebuilt and raised a few inches. It would be well worth your while to do so. On the other hand, if the oarlock position seems so high that you have to reach up too much while making oar strokes, add a seat cushion to raise the rower's position.

Foot braces matched to your height and leg length are important—much of your rowing power comes from your legs. If foot braces are absent or not ideally located, rig them up to fit you perfectly.

Nonslip traction is important for standing fishermen. Most boats now come with rough-textured floors under the knee brace position. These can wear smooth, though. Add traction strips or a rubber mat whenever you start to slip. It's not unusual for anglers to slip and fall out of the back of the boat. It happens every so often and could be dangerous on trickier stretches of water. An older angler slipped, fell, and hit his head on the gunwale before falling in the river and drowning last year in my neighborhood. This accident demonstrates that unexpected tragedies can occur in float fishing. The right boat and proper rigging help prevent such disasters.

Some rowers like to add high-back seats for their position. These are offered as price-added options by many manufacturers. Theoretically, this interferes with rowing a bit, but guides who spend many days and long hours on a stream find the added back support desirable.

Rod holders of some sort are preferred if not built in. Most are rigged just under the gunwales on the inside of the boat using Velcro, hooks of some kind, or a PVC tube.

Most drift-boat models are designed for fly fishing these days. Many traditional West Coast drifters were designed to have two spin, plug, or bait anglers fish from the front seat, while back trolling with no one in the back. You'll see some with two front-seat backrests. Some 14-foot or shorter models have no back seat at all. Even though I'd much rather row one angler than two any day, note how the seats are rigged on boats you're considering. Those geared for fly fishing should have front and rear seat positions with knee braces. There should be low line-tangle potential in the design. Watch for rough edges or bolts on older boats that could tear waders. Consider side height in terms of performance needed and wind resistance. Length, width, and weight vary, too. These could be important to those wishing to float small or rampless rivers.

One modification I made to my drift-boat trailer was to build a motorcycle ramp on the front for doing my own shuttles. This calls for a longer tongue, a built-in hinged loading ramp,

The self-contained angler takes a light motorcycle (a bike would also do) for doing his own shuttle. This way, you don't have to take a second vehicle or depend on fly shop hours.

and tie-down positions. The axle position might need to be changed on some trailers so that you can still lift the tongue with ease. A wheel-fitted rolling tongue-lifter makes it possible to hitch up your boat with a light cycle on it. I had mine built with a cycle rack from the start, so balance wasn't a problem. Obviously, very light motorcycles are preferred, from scooters to trail bikes of the smallest sizes. These provide inexpensive self-shuttling options—you won't need to pay shuttle fees or plan around a fly shop's business hours. There are places where no shuttles are readily available. Rain, snow, and dense riverside hatches make cycle shuttles less than amusing at times, so bring a helmet with a face shield! I try to shuttle in the mornings, at the beginning of the trip, to get it over with and try to avoid major bug hatches. You never know what evening weather will bring, and the bugs are sure to be thicker then.

A boat cover is a good investment and a must for a wooden boat. Covers protect finishes and color while also keeping water from collecting in the bottom of your boat. Although drift boats do have drain plugs (don't forget to put them back in!), it's added work to have to drain a boat before use. It can be almost impossible to lift the tongue to tilt and drain it if it is very full of water. Some drift-boat trailers are built to tilt, allowing boats to drain. Water sitting in the bottom of a boat can discolor it and age oars and life jackets left there. A cover may keep the casual thief from walking off with your accessories, too. Most hitches can be locked, making it difficult for someone to hitch up your boat and drive off with it.

One other little accessory that is handy in some situations is an oar holder. This is nothing more than a piece of PVC pipe that slides over the handle of one oar. It should not be much wider than the diameter of the oar. When you stop to drag a boat over a gravel bar on a shallow river (which is something I do a lot) or just to tie on a fly, the tube is slid over both oar handles. This keeps them parallel and lifted up out of the water.

It's particularly practical with pin and clip oar arrangements when the rower wants to jump in and out of the boat. In other cases, you can just let your oars trail in the water or pull them in and across the boat. You can paint the PVC tube to match your boat if you like, which looks better than the plumbing motif.

No matter what kind of boat you choose, attention to detail will add to your enjoyment. There are boats on the market that row better than others, handle big water or wind better than others, or have better or more storage. Some knee braces and adjustable seats are more comfortable, and some oars feel better in the water. Shop around and try to row as many varieties of boat as you can before investing in one. You're likely to find one that fits your style, your river, and your local float-fishing needs.

7

Planning Your Trip

Good planning is desirable for day trips and essential for well-run, longer expeditions. A meeting of minds is in order to plan everything from departure times to equipment needs, meals, food preservation, camp setups, fly selection, and so on. I find lists to be of great help, so I don't forget the details (like coffee, toilet paper, and rum). Extra straps used to secure rafts to trailers can help tie down tarps at camp. You need to think through everything, down to the dog's food and bowl.

ESSENTIAL GEAR
In addition to fishing tackle, some things that I find essential include a large boat net and rod cases that also house reels to protect rods that aren't in use. Hemostats or needle-nose pliers are handy for removing flies from fish, anchor ropes, and certain parts of the human anatomy. Don't forget raingear, hot- and cold-weather clothing, hat, sunglasses, sunscreen, lip balm, skin cream (days on arid and windy western rivers can really take it out of your skin), insect repellent, plus adequate

nourishment and liquid refreshment. Have plenty of drinking water on hand for very hot days.

A good waterproof duffel bag is best for storing gear. Those with lengthwise openings are much easier to get in and out of than the old narrow-end-sealing whitewater bags. Avoid duffels with excess buckles, straps, and other appendages that fly line gets caught around. Manufacturers haven't even thought about this aspect of in-boat gear. Waders are good not only for insulated wading but also as raingear during cold thunderstorms (or summer snowstorms). I usually wear shorts and sandals in the boat and carry boot-foot waders for deep wading or rain. These are easy to get into and out of.

Life jackets, a first-aid kit and book, an extra oar, and throw rope should be on hand when you are floating, plus a patch kit and pump for rafts. A detailed river map is helpful if the rower is unfamiliar with the water: These are available for most rivers these days. Flashlights come in handy for late take-outs. Do have a spare set of keys for your shuttle vehicles! Don't forget to make your shuttle arrangements at the beginning of your trip.

In cold weather, a thermos or two of hot soup or drink helps take the chill off. A small stove and hot lunch is a good idea, too. Prepared meals can be brought along. Have some fire starter and matches or a lighter in case of hypothermia. Extra raincoats and gloves are good to keep stowed on board.

High-quality waterproof containers are widely available for cameras, first-aid kits, fire-starting gear, glasses, wallets, books, cell phones, and what have you. You might want to bring an extra camera battery along, too—it might be a big-fish day!

Being prepared for any contingency is a little more work but a lot more satisfying than having your day ruined by inattention to detail. Forgetting raingear on a long day of cold rain or neglecting to bring sunscreen on sunny days can create negative memories of float trips for novice floaters.

SHUTTLES AND SUCH

Shuttles are a necessary evil of float fishing. Once I bought a motorboat so I could park at the take-out, run upstream early (when there was no one around to tick off), and then float all day back to the ramp. That was a $12,000 shuttle.

Typically, you either take two vehicles (one can be a bicycle, scooter, four-wheeler, or the like) or pay a fly shop to do your shuttle. With fly shop shuttles, you'll stop at a shop to pay for them to move your vehicle for you, giving them your vehicle description, license plate number, an extra key, and telling them where and when you want your vehicle shuttled. If you don't take an extra key, you need to hide your key someplace, tell them where to find it, and have them return it there after the shuttle. Fly shops often run their shuttles midday, after the morning business rush.

It's a good idea to have your car shuttled at least a couple hours before you actually plan to take out. They could run late. A storm could come up, someone could get sunburned, or a tailwind could shove you down the river early. These days, when everyone has a cell phone, you can call from the river to make changes, if you do it early enough.

I have three sets of keys for my vehicle. I keep one in my boat storage, one in a fishing box, and the third in my pocket so that I never end up at a take-out without a key. (It happens quite often with beginners.) Besides those keys, three fly shops each have a key for doing my shuttles.

Some shops don't open very early, though they may have a drop box for early key drops, payment, and instructions. Otherwise, you have to call the day before and put it on a credit card, or you have to wait till they open, which is not good if you want to get an early start.

When doing shuttles yourself, you need two vehicles. Sure, you can hitchhike the shuttle, but that can take a long time. Sometimes I fish a short stretch but fish it hard. When with family or friends, I might walk that shuttle for exercise, while they rig the fishing gear. I drop the boat and crew off at the put-in, drive the truck to the take-out, and walk back to the launch. (You can ride a bicycle, too.) By doing your shuttle early, you can often get a better parking spot for your rig and trailer, one that allows an easier ramp approach at the end of the day.

On longer shuttles, I put the boat in (anchor it securely, away from the ramp while you're gone) and then drive my rig and trailer to the take-out, with the second vehicle following. I park my vehicle at the take-out and then drive back to the put-in in the second car. At the end of the day, you load the boat and then go back upstream to pick up that second vehicle. It's wise to leave someone with the boat while you're gone on shuttles.

The other way to do this is to drop a second vehicle at the take-out on your way upstream to the put-in. When done floating, you drive the second vehicle upstream to pick up the trailering rig. Then you drive back downstream and pull the boat out. Make sure all drivers have their keys! In either case, shuttles are two-part deals, before and after the float.

At one time, I had a motorcycle ramp built onto my trailer. I would do my motorcycle shuttle early, while traffic and bugs were thin. I'd have my truck and trailer waiting at the take-out when I got there. This is cheaper than taking two vehicles a long way from town. These do-it-yourself shuttles can add an extra 45 minutes or more of downtime to your day. Between the downtime and gas for the second vehicle, it can be cheaper and easier to hire a shuttle.

Shuttle drivers aren't all angels, though. Some drive fast, dirt road or not, especially if they have a lot of shuttles to do. Once in a rare while, they'll damage or even wreck cars. I leave a note on the driver's seat verifying the take-out location, telling them to put my sun shade up, and asking them to drive easy. If you use a shuttle service often, a tip now and then might help ensure good vehicle treatment.

Vehicles are occasionally broken into at accesses. Thieves know you're gone for the day. Don't leave valuables lying around in plain view. Don't leave anything behind if you don't have to, or at least cover it up.

A few other pointers: It may be possible to avoid the busiest times at ramps by going a little earlier or later. Some accesses are madhouses at predictable hours. Certain ramps can accommodate two or even three vehicles side by side. If so, don't hog the whole thing. Put in and get out quickly. At the end of the day, clean your waders off a bit before throwing them in someone's vehicle, as they can splatter a lot of mud. And with today's concern about transporting exotic species, it's a good idea to wash both waders and boat at home and let them dry thoroughly before hitting the next river. Finally, don't wear wading cleats in boats!

WHITEWATER CLASS RATINGS

As a fisherman, you may not be interested in whitewater, but if someone mentions that a river is class IV, you better know what that means! Underestimating rivers and overestimating rowing skills leads to many river trip disasters. The following explanation of the internationally accepted whitewater rating system, which defines water in classes, from class I to class VI, will give you a good foundation. Knowing what these ratings mean will help you plan for the type of water you are likely to encounter on your trip.

Western rivers often feature miles of easier class I to III water, with the occasional class IV or V rapid here and there. Big rapids can be scouted and run or portaged around, although carrying heavy boating equipment over piles of boulders isn't much fun! Boaters may line an empty boat through a tight spot. This requires at least two long ropes of, say, 50 feet attached to each end. They may need to be snugged off on rocks or trees to manage the boat's momentum. As always, good judgment is

Class I rivers are basically flat water, but what's around the corner? Class II or III spots could be encountered. River maps, fish and game departments, and fly shops can help you plan your trip.

key. Maps, research, word of mouth, and close observation help; then add more good judgment.

Class I
Mellow, essentially flat-moving water. All rivers have some dangers, though, such as bridge pilings, diversion dams, log-jams, and powerful eddy lines. High water or obstacles can bump this classification up a notch or two. Class I is safe for all craft in knowledgeable hands.

Class II
More current, swift with some waves and rocks to dodge. Holes and sharp eddy lines could overturn small craft like canoes and johnboats (in the wrong hands). Not "technical" by whitewater standards (meaning there are open, straightforward chutes to

go through), class II requires observation, alertness, and rowing skills. Rafts are more forgiving than other craft, but drift boats, pontoon craft, and prams usually have no problem with class IIs. Float tubes should see this as their upper limit. Learning rowers should start out on class Is and IIs before progressing to class IIIs. Back rowing, quick pivot turns, and ferrying should all become second nature by then. Note that a class II with a diversion dam or logjam can still be a killer.

Class III

Class III rivers have obvious rapids in places. These can include boulder gardens to weave through, waves to 6 feet, holes that can flip boats, and sharp bends with tricky crosscurrents and whirlpools. To a whitewater paddler, class IIIs are just fun, bouncing rapids, with relatively easy chutes through. Experienced rowers with good-size boats (13 to 17 feet) have few

Class III rivers have obvious rapids, waves, and rock gardens. Whitewater paddlers view this as easy water, but there is the potential to flip fishing boats and lose gear, or even life, especially if a beginner is at the oars.

problems with them, though you may want to scout rapids first, secure gear, and put on life jackets. Flips do happen here, in holes and against boulders, even with old hands at the oars, if your attention is distracted or you blow an oar (knock it out of place by hitting a rock).

Learning rowers should stop, scout, and discuss rowing routes before proceeding. Everyone should wear a life jacket when a beginner is at the oars and for all water class III and up (or anytime you wouldn't want to swim). Children are required to wear life jackets at all times in most states. Class III is about as much water as most fishermen will want to handle. Beyond this, the chance of a flip, swim, and lost gear go way up!

Class IV
Now we're in serious rapids, the kind where you might hear thunder around the corner, see mist in the air, and watch the river drop out of view. Most fishermen don't want to mess with class IVs, but whitewater enthusiasts who like to fish will. On some western steelhead rivers, class IVs are run with caution all the time.

Class IV rapids feature boulder-congested routes where no easy way through is to be seen. There are big boat-flipping holes, waves to 10 feet, and a lot of white froth (which means you don't float much, even in a life jacket). Boat flips are fairly common in class IVs, so all gear needs to be lashed down, loose ropes coiled and harnessed, and fishing rods kept in a good grip! Tighten your life jacket. Should you go for a swim, assume that horizontal backstroking position we discussed, with your feet up to fend off rocks. Never try to stand up in rapids. Feel free to walk around rapids that scare you. A lighter boat makes it easier for the rower to maneuver. This will be the limit for average-size drift boats (in very experienced hands only). Large rafts and big pontoon boats (over 14 feet) may proceed with caution onto class V.

Class IV rapids call for skilled rowers and scouting. Waves to ten feet, turbulent boulder gardens, and killer holes can be encountered. Wear life jackets, secure gear, and be ready for action.

Class V

These are like class IVs on steroids. Extreme boulder congestion, big drops and even waterfalls, killer holes that will eat you in the blink of an eye, waves to 20 feet—you get the idea. Anglers with lots of nice equipment to lose rarely want to take on class Vs or even class IVs. Boats often flip here, even if the rower is an old pro. What the others do in the boat, which way they lean, and how well they hold on can all affect a successful run through menacing rapids. Big rafts of 16 to 18 feet, rowed by a pro, can be safe enough. Kayakers may float through like butterflies, but angling parties probably don't belong here.

Class VI

Class VI means unrunnable on the international scale. It's pretty self-explanatory. Most people won't even want to stand on the edge!

Some anglers won't want to mess with class IV and V rivers, but seasoned floaters with the right equipment enjoy the challenge, and some whitewater stretches don't get much fishing pressure.

SCOUTING TROUBLE SPOTS

Any time you come up to a questionable spot, stop to scout it. Things to watch and listen for include sharp bends with no views downstream, dull to loud roars, logjams and boulder gardens, clean drops (including diversion dams), and low bridges.

Not only do you want to stop to scout, you want to stop upstream far enough to be able to position the boat anywhere across the river when you start again. Your boat position, angle, and setup can be the key to a successful run, even before you actually get to the rapid.

You may want to stop 100 feet upstream on a mellow river or a quarter of a mile in advance on a turbulent one. Stopping too close to an obstacle may not give you enough setup time when you take off again. Err on the cautious side. You'll want a long rope to tie the boat off on a rock or tree while you walk downstream and look the hazard over. (Long ropes are also used to line boats around rapids and to pull wrapped ones off boulders.)

Look for the best route through and for landmarks to position yourself by. The view from midriver and midrapid can look completely different from the one you just had from an elevated bank. After memorizing a route and landmarks, walk back upstream, tighten your life jackets, stow and secure the rope, and row the boat over to the best entry lane of the rapid.

At this point, a skilled rower may utilize the preplanned route perfectly. On the other hand, he may have to use his quick instincts to adjust to a new situation. An oar blown out by a shallow, unlooked-for rock can completely change your plans. You can bounce off boulders and go the wrong way. A quick pivot and decision will now have to be made in an instant. When rowing becomes second nature, most such problems are overcome. If a beginner has to stop and think about whether he should push or pull on which oar, bad things can happen quickly.

There may be times when the rower will want to take a boat through a tight rapid alone. (It could be the fisherman's idea, too.) Humans weigh a lot. An empty boat is much lighter and easier to maneuver. Most times, though, routes will be straightforward enough for a skilled rower. Live by the old river adage, "If in doubt, scout!"

EXPEDITION RIGGING

A little experience with day floats on scenic Western waterways usually leads to an interest in multiday camping expeditions. Many famous trout and steelhead rivers offer overnight trips. Some are permit rivers requiring advance planning (as long as a year in advance) with federal or state agencies. Other, less famous rivers can be float-camped, too, which adds another level of adventure and relaxation (some states' laws are more tolerant than others when it comes to river-corridor use).

River camps require good planning. Camp gear, food and water, emergency supplies, boats, and fishing gear all need to be thought out. A comfortable setup provides great streamside experiences.

There's little to match the enjoyment of camping on the edge of a beautiful mountain river, watching the sunset, hitting the evening hatches, and then eating a hearty camp meal with a good bottle of wine. Evenings, nights, and dawns are intriguing times to be on a stream, rather than worrying about making it to the take-out and on down the road.

Overnight trips and extended expeditions usually require a boat at least 14 feet long for two or more people. A solo boater could get by with a 12 foot or even smaller boat. Rafts handle big loads better than drift boats and draw less water. A heavily loaded drift boat can draw over a foot of water, taking some hard-hitting hull abuse on shallower rocky rivers. Self-bailing rafts are the best all-around choice if you see many overnighters in your floating future. Many groups take one large raft with all the camp gear and no passengers, in addition to the fishing boats.

AN EXPEDITION-EQUIPPED FISHING RAFT

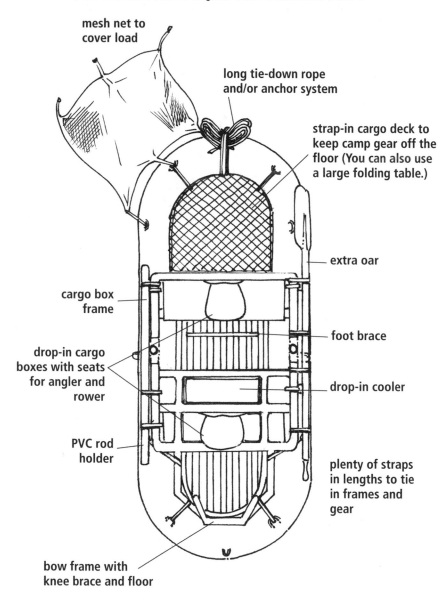

mesh net to cover load

long tie-down rope and/or anchor system

strap-in cargo deck to keep camp gear off the floor (You can also use a large folding table.)

extra oar

cargo box frame

foot brace

drop-in cargo boxes with seats for angler and rower

drop-in cooler

PVC rod holder

plenty of straps in lengths to tie in frames and gear

bow frame with knee brace and floor

A 14- to 16-foot boat allows plenty of camping luxuries. This ain't no backpacking trip! Thoughtful planning can include comforts while covering the necessities plus emergency supplies. Having spent the last 20 years doing three- to seven-day campout trips on Montana's Smith River has allowed me to get in tune with expedition packing and cooking. Both take plenty of forethought to do well. At the end of this chapter are checklists that you can use to help plan your own expeditions. The following provides an overview of one outfitter's camp setup.

Big tarps are very handy. They are the heart of our camps. We use extra-strong custom-made ones of about 20 by 20 feet. Smaller ones will do for camps of two to six people. Days and nights of rain (or snow) are no fun without a big tarp. Cooking and standing around in the rain or in a small tent gets old after a while. Another option some outfitters use is a large wall tent. This is a bulkier and more elaborate setup.

Big tarps give protection from both rain and sun. This is important on those trips during blistering summer heat waves. Big tarps keep campers and food coolers shaded, prolonging the life of ice and fresh foods. Tarps are also used to cover the boat's load. They can be folded to shape and placed over a load before netting or tying down. (The camp load on a raft is usually confined to the back half, which leaves the front half for anglers. One big tarp can cover all the gear.) This protects your equipment from rain during the floating day and can lessen the need for so many costly waterproof bags where big whitewater isn't an issue.

The biggest problem with tarps is wind. Our fierce Montana winds can destroy all but the best-set camps from time to time. Wind will rip the grommets out of cheap tarps (you can then tie knots in the corners or use the old "rock wrapped in the tarp" tie-down method). Stakes will come flying out of the ground in a big or sudden blow. The best stakes we've come up with are 2- to 3-foot sections of conduit. These can be driven into most kinds of ground and gravel with a big hammer or ax butt. They can also be taken back out easily enough. They hold very well when deeply sunk and properly angled, and they last a long time. Those cheap plastic and small wood or iron stakes aren't worth a hoot when it comes to tarping. Don't cut green wood off trees, either. This is now looked down upon along our heavily used river corridors. Firewood becomes scarce, and people hack green trees for no good reason. Campsites can become shabby looking. If you do need a fire or stake wood (where it's legal), look for it at midday when floating between camps, not at them. It's much easier to find that way.

We always stake out tarps in readiness for the biggest storms at each camp, using trees as tie-downs whenever possible. The long conduit stakes work well on treeless tarp corners, and we use long ropes and oars to keep the tarp at the right height for us to walk under. Ropes at least 30 feet long should be attached to each corner, with four extra ones on hand to reinforce the side midpoints. Sometimes we double-stake corners if the ground is soft or the position seems shaky. Ropes are set along the sides to tighten the tarp like a drum. It's much better to be overstaked than understaked when that big thunderstorm hits! Sudden gusts of 60 mph are not uncommon. I hate to have prepared a complex dinner and then have the tarp blow away, knocking down the entire kitchen and dumping the food in the dirt!

The guides usually sleep under the tarp on cots or on the ground. Our guests stay in tents that are far enough away so as not to hear us snore (or vice versa). Though even the best-laid tarp has blown away on occasion and even collapsed under the weight of heavy nighttime snow (a rude awakening), for the most part, tarps have given us decades of cooking and sleeping shelter.

Any design of tent can be brought along to match your personality and the size of your boat. There are plenty of choices, from the smallest, lightest backpacking models to roomy 12-by-12 foot or larger models that you can stand up and even cook in. Your choice in float-and-camp gear reflects how much comfort you desire versus how much time you want to spend hauling it around, setting it up, and tearing it down. The young often prefer strip-down lightweight camps, which also cost less. Many older floaters have come to appreciate the comforts of a table and chair, a tent you can stand up to enter, and a well-padded cot.

In spring and fall, when the potential for cold mornings and evenings is high, big tents make good cookhouses and dining areas. Stoves and lanterns heat a tent quickly, giving it a homey ambience. Cold wind, which otherwise sucks the heat right out of a meal, is blocked, along with rain, bugs, or snow. You must have some ventilation, though, to allow fumes to disperse. Such large tents need to be securely staked out, too, and even roped down. I've seen one blow across a meadow with one very surprised woman still inside!

Chairs and tables are great comforts when one is spending days on the river. Whittling at a steak with a paper plate on your lap while sitting on the ground just doesn't do it. There are plenty of portable collapsing models around to choose from.

For cooking and preparing food, you'll want sturdier tables built to working height so you don't have to bend over to slice and dice. These are available from specialty river equipment dealers and catalogs, generally in the whitewater market, such as Northwest River Supply. They're rather pricey but worthwhile on stream if many riverside days are in your future. You could build one yourself, as river bums are apt to do. They can be designed to fit across the back of your raft as a loading platform for camp gear, and thus must be sturdily constructed.

There are plenty of waterproof bag and box options around these days to carry dry goods and duffel. Traditionally, whitewater enthusiasts required totally waterproof containers in case of flips. Some of these were expensive or heavy. Most fishing floaters don't expect to flip or get drenched by big waves, though. They can get by with the larger household storage containers sold in discount stores and the waterproof bags now found in most outdoor-product catalogs. Specialty river equipment catalogs will fill you in on the best, most rugged, and highest-tech gear. Tie in or net over your gear securely when floating, though, to keep from losing it overboard during collisions with boulders and such. Nothing of value should be able to wash free, even in a flip. Ultimately, everything should be tied, strapped, or netted.

Some permit rivers have special regulations. Fires may not be allowed, or you may be required to take a fire plan. In extreme cases (like the Grand Canyon, which does have some big trout), you even have to pack out all human waste. In such cases, special equipment can be required by the permitting agency, and it will be inspected at the put-in site.

Cooking on the river varies from the most basic to gourmet. You can make just about anything, with the right planning, equipment, and perhaps a little advance preparation at home. It's almost as easy to prepare some great dishes as it is simple ones. River folk always appreciate that extra effort, especially at mealtime. Everything does seem to taste better riverside after a long day of fishing.

On longer expeditions, taking care of your coolers, food, and ice becomes a concern. There are tricks of the trade that help, and foods that last longer than others. Block ice, two to three blocks per large cooler, kept stacked together, lasts up to five days if people aren't continually opening and closing the cooler, and if it's babied throughout the trip. Meats, juices, bread, and such for the later days of the trip should be frozen beforehand to prolong their cooler life. (On cool-weather trips, this won't be necessary, and you might even have trouble defrosting frozen foods.)

Getting ready to break camp on Montana's South Fork of the Flathead. Some wilderness rivers require permits, which need to be applied for up to a year in advance. Going with an outfitter who already has the permit is another option.

Keep coolers out of direct sunlight at all times. Cover them when they are in the boat, and put them in the shade of a tarp as soon as you reach camp. This is the first thing I do after setting up a tarp. As the sun crosses the sky and the tarp shadow moves, relocate coolers to keep them shaded.

We have one trick that really helps to stretch ice life to five or more days. We soak large, thick white beach or bath towels with water and cover each cooler with them. They are rewetted in the river whenever they begin to dry. Thick white towels hold moisture a long time and act like air conditioners. You can feel an appreciable difference between the air temperature of other items in your boat compared with the wetted cooler—I'd guess 20 to 30 degrees. We keep wet towels on coolers in the shade of the tarp, too, every moment of the day. This adds one to three days of life to ice, making a major difference in preserving fresh foods during hot-weather trips.

When loading coolers at the start, we pack the block ice on the cooler bottoms bunched together. Frozen foods go in next, along with other stuff that won't crush. Lighter and fragile items go on top. In coolers other than those with fresh, fragile produce, we spread cube ice over the tops to fill in gaps. A custom-cut piece of bubble wrap or other sheet insulation adds more ice protection. Such a cooler kept covered with a wet towel and seldom opened will hold ice a long time.

Some outfitters on very long trips will have coolers packed for day-by-day use. They'll even duct-tape coolers closed to seal out hot summer air. We usually categorize coolers by meat, dairy, vegetable and fruit, and drink. In this way, meat blood is kept out of cheese, fresh fruit and vegetables aren't crushed and spoiled by heavy objects and too much ice contact, and coolers that people open and close the most—drink coolers—aren't compromising meats and other foods because their ice is melting.

Making sure everything, including canned drinks, is well chilled before going into coolers helps immensely, too. Adding cans of drinks at room temperature to ice immediately begins to melt it. Proper attention to these details will make ice last throughout your trip. We sometimes take an ice cooler filled with nothing but block and cube ice, especially if the crew is fond of cocktails on ice come evening. For extra-long expeditions, you can add dry ice atop an ice cooler and tape it shut.

Some foods last better than others. For instance, strawberries tend to mold after a couple of days. Fish needs to be perfectly wrapped. Tomatoes are likely to get smashed if you don't constantly relocate them to the top of the cooler after digging around for other foods. Plan to use fragile and quick-spoiling items early in the trip, and save longer-lasting things like frozen meat, celery, and potatoes for the last days. Some fruits and vegetables, such as potatoes, onions, cantaloupes, apples, and oranges, don't need to be kept on ice at all. They can be kept in a dry box in the shade or covered with a wet towel.

Of course, you could dispense with fresh foods altogether and just take canned and prepackaged stuff and a few hunks of meat, pasta, and rice. There are better canned alternatives these days, with better spicing and less sugar and salt. Many dry packaged goods have become tastier, too. Freeze-dried backpacking meals are always an option, although they don't seem overly popular with floaters. Cooking alternatives are plentiful.

We favor propane kitchens using several two- to three-burner stoves and lanterns. There are also oven and barbecue grill propane accessories. A large propane tank will give us a good week of steady use.

Some floaters are into Dutch oven cooking, which opens up many baking possibilities, including cakes, casseroles, muffins, and the like. These are fueled by charcoal briquettes. Light-load trippers might prefer one-burner backpacking or two-burner fuel stoves. This will depend on your temperament, party size, length of trip, and preference, or lack thereof, for good food. Many guide operations and private floaters delve deep into the gourmet world on river trips. The surprise of outstanding meals and fine wines heightens the overall trip experience. To others, hot dogs, baked beans, and beer represent the true camping experience. As long as I get full at the end of a long rowing day, I'm happy!

The following checklists are taken from the years of guiding I've done with Montana River Outfitters. These could be more extensive than you might want, but most options are covered. We usually end up with a four- to six-page checklist for our guided expeditions on Montana's Smith, South Fork of the Flathead, and other regional rivers. You can photocopy and edit these to meet your floating needs.

Float-Fishing Checklists

DRIFT BOAT AND PRAM LIST

___ anchor and rope
___ boat and trailer
___ boat cover
___ boat net
___ camera and video
___ check light hookups
___ cooler with ice
___ drain plugs
___ drinks
___ extra clothes for all
weather conditions
___ extra keys
___ extra water
___ first-aid kit
___ fishing license
___ flashlight
___ flies
___ food
___ guidebooks
___ hat
___ insect repellent
___ life jackets

___ lunch storage box
___ lunch utensils
___ maps
___ oarlocks
___ oars
___ oar tube
___ personal duffel
___ raingear
___ rods and reels
___ rowing gloves
___ seat cushions
___ shuttle arrangements
___ stove and fuel
___ sunglasses
___ sunscreen and lip balm
___ tackle
___ throw rope
___ waders
___ waterproof bags
___ waterproof camera box
___ other:

RAFT SUPPLEMENT

___ cargo deck and netting
___ drop-in boxes
___ patch kit

___ pumps (electric and
manual)
___ raft

___ rod holder
___ rowing frame(s)
___ seats

___ straps and tie-downs
___ other:

OVERNIGHT-TRIP SUPPLEMENT

___ ax (can be used as hammer for stakes)
___ big tarp with ropes attached and 4 to 8 stakes
___ biodegradable soap
___ buckets
___ cameras and film
___ candles
___ cargo decks and nets
___ chairs
___ charcoal
___ clothes for all weather conditions
___ coolers
___ cots
___ dining table
___ dishwashing supplies
___ dry goods boxes
___ Dutch oven
___ emergency radio
___ expanded first-aid kit
___ extra keys
___ extra rods
___ extra straps and tie-downs

___ 50-foot rope (to tie up boats at night and for wraps)
___ fire starter
___ fishing gear
___ flashlights
___ fly-tying kit
___ food and drink
___ garbage bags
___ grill for pit cooking
___ ice
___ insect repellent
___ kitchen box
___ lantern and mantles
___ lighter fluid
___ matches and lighters
___ menu
___ mirror
___ pads and mattresses
___ paper cups
___ personal medications
___ personal toilet kit
___ personal washing bowl
___ pillow
___ portable toilet
___ propane barbecue grill

Float-Fishing Checklists, continued

___ propane hookups
___ propane oven
___ propane tanks
___ raingear
___ saw
___ shovel
___ shuttle arrangements
___ skin cream
___ sleeping bags
___ solar shower
___ stoves and fuel
___ sunscreen
___ tablecloth

___ tables for stove and kitchen
___ tents and stakes
___ thermos
___ toilet paper
___ tools and extra propane hoses
___ video camera
___ water containers
___ water filter
___ waterproof bags
___ waterproof boxes
___ white towels
___ other:

KITCHEN BOX EQUIPMENT

___ aluminum foil
___ bleach
___ bottle opener
___ bowls
___ can opener
___ carafe and thermos
___ chef knives
___ coffee, teas
___ coffee cups
___ coffeepot
___ condiments
___ cooking oils
___ corkscrew
___ creamer

___ cutting boards
___ dish-draining rack
___ dish rags and towels
___ dish soap (biodegradable)
___ dish tub
___ drinking glasses
___ Dutch oven
___ flashlight
___ frying pans
___ garbage bags
___ grater
___ griddle
___ hot chocolate

___ hot pads
___ kitchen first-aid kit
___ ladle
___ large fork
___ large mixing bowls
___ large soup pot
___ marinades
___ matches and lighter
___ menu
___ napkins
___ paper cups
___ paper towels
___ pitcher
___ plates
___ salt and pepper
___ saucepans
___ scrubber
___ self-sealing plastic bags
___ serving platter
___ serving spoons

___ sharpening steel
___ shish kebab sticks
___ silverware
___ spatulas
___ spices
___ steak knives
___ steamer
___ sugar and sugar
    substitute
___ syrup and jellies
___ tablecloth
___ tongs
___ tools for propane and
    camp work
___ toothpicks
___ vegetable peeler
___ water filter with tablets
___ other:

BASIC EXTENDED-TRIP SHOPPING LIST

Staples
___ aluminum foil
___ baking powder
___ bleach
___ boxed meals
    (e.g., macaroni and
    cheese)
___ canned foods
___ cereals
___ chocolate bars

___ cookies
___ cooking chocolate
___ cooking oils
___ corn chips
___ corn starch
___ crackers
___ dish soap
___ dried fruit
___ flour
___ garbage bags

Float-Fishing Checklists, continued

___ honey
___ jellies
___ ketchup
___ marinades
___ matches
___ mayonnaise
___ mustards
___ pancake mix
___ paper towels
___ pasta
___ pickles
___ potato chips
___ pretzels
___ rice
___ salad dressings
___ salsa
___ salt and pepper
___ sauce and gravy mixes
___ self-sealing plastic bags
___ spices for menu
___ sugar and sugar
     substitute
___ syrups
___ Tabasco
___ toilet paper
___ other:

Drinks
___ beer
___ bottled waters

___ coffee and teas
___ hot chocolate
___ juices
___ liquors (drinking and
     cooking)
___ milk
___ powdered drink mix
___ sodas
___ wine
___ other:

Meats
Breakfast Meats
___ bacon
___ Canadian bacon
___ ham
___ sausage
___ steaks
___ other:

Lunch Meats
___ corned beef
___ fried chicken
___ ham
___ pastrami
___ roast beef
___ salami
___ smoked turkey

___ turkey
___ other:

Dinner Meats
___ chicken
___ Cornish game hens
___ fish
___ lamb
___ pork chops and loins
___ shish kebab beef
___ shrimp
___ steaks
___ other:

Vegetables
___ asparagus
___ broccoli
___ carrots
___ cauliflower
___ celery
___ corn
___ cucumbers
___ garlic
___ green peppers
___ hash browns
___ herbs
___ hot peppers
___ lettuce
___ onions
___ potatoes
___ red peppers

___ shallots
___ snow peas
___ spinach
___ tomatoes
___ other:

Fruit
___ apples
___ avocados
___ bananas
___ berries
___ canned fruit
___ cantaloupes
___ frozen fruit
___ grapes
___ lemons
___ limes
___ melons
___ oranges
___ pears
___ pineapples
___ plums
___ strawberries
___ other:

Dairy
___ butter
___ cream
___ cream cheese
___ eggs and/or egg
    substitute

Float-Fishing Checklists, continued

___ margarine
___ milks
___ sour cream
___ whipped cream

Cheeses
___ blue
___ Cheddar
___ jack
___ Parmesan
___ Swiss
___ other:

Breads
___ bagels
___ cakes
___ cheese rolls
___ cookies
___ croissants
___ dinner rolls
___ English muffins
___ fajita shells
___ French bread
___ kaiser rolls
___ onion rolls
___ pies
___ pita bread
___ poor boys
___ pound cake

___ sandwich bread
___ other:

Etc.
___ charcoal
___ first-aid supplies
___ fishing licenses
___ flies
___ fuel for vehicles
___ ice
___ lantern mantles
___ lighter fluid
___ propane
___ shuttle and permit fees
___ stove fuel
___ other:

It's not unusual to have one or more people on a trip who eat only low-fat foods, are vegetarians, or are allergic to certain foods. Some are on medications, are allergic to bee stings, have heart conditions, or what have you. It helps to be aware of these things in advance on longer expeditions.

Although preparing for a long expedition is a major chore in itself and one not to be underestimated, the comforts on-stream make good planning worthwhile. If all share evenly in the planning, loading, rowing, camp cooking, dishwashing, camp breakdown, shuttling, trip unloading, and equipment cleanup, things will go quickly and smoothly. Those who stand around while others do the work or who don't show up to load and unload tend not to be asked on future expeditions. Making sure there's no clash of personalities at the onset helps ensure enjoyable trips, too. These are no small matters. Eventually, small cadres of voyagers tend to click. Many travel together over decades down North America's or the world's best rivers and fisheries. It would take more than a lifetime to experience them all. I know many a river addict, old and young.

8

Trailering, Ramp Use, and River Etiquette

To those who spend a lot of time on rivers and boat ramps, the unwritten rules of the game become a code to operate by. The inexperienced sometimes don't have a clue as to why others might be irritated with them. There are proper ways to do things in keeping harmony on the river.

Life at a boat ramp these days isn't quite as pleasant as it was 20 years ago, when no one else was likely to be around. There can be regular traffic jams at popular boat ramps now. Unloading and loading procedures should be streamlined to speed up ramp use. The following are some hints on keeping ramp tension down.

First, load and unload quickly; then get your vehicle out of the way. Don't park on the ramp drinking coffee and tying on flies if others are waiting to use it. If you are in line waiting to use the ramp, use that time to load your fishing gear into the boat and untie it (except for the winch at the bow) so that when your turn comes you can quickly push your boat off the trailer into the river and pull the vehicle away. It is particularly irritating to wait on those who choose to inflate and rig or deflate a raft on the ramp itself, instead of doing this off to one side and then using the ramp when the raft is rigged. Some unthinking people also park in such a fashion as to block the approach to the ramp, not taking into consideration how much space a trailering vehicle needs to operate.

After getting your boat in the water, move it away from the ramp itself. Tie it up or anchor it where it's not in any other boat's way. Don't park it right next to someone else's boat, where it's going to repeatedly bump into it. Treat other people's boats like gold. New and wooden-boat owners are likely to be hostile to someone who mindlessly slams a boat into theirs. Some unthinking floaters with older craft will let their boats frequently bump against others at launch sites. You wouldn't do it with your car, so don't do it with your boat. Try to park it well away from others, pull it up on the bank, or have someone hold it in place so currents and wind don't slam it into another craft. If you go off for a long shuttle and leave your boat in the river, park well away from the ramp. Have someone stay with the boat in case it needs to be moved or held in place. This also helps avert theft, which is all too common these days, even along backcountry rivers. I've also seen unattended parked boats get blown away by strong winds.

When loading back up at the end of the day, get your boat on the trailer and then quickly pull the vehicle away. Don't sit there blocking the ramp while unrigging rods, taking off waders, and drinking a beer. Streamlining and minimizing your ramp-use time makes the floating day more enjoyable for everyone: Remember that some people might have to drive a couple of hundred miles after getting off the river. A parade of slothlike floater take-outs naturally irritates those who have to get somewhere and don't want to fall asleep at the wheel along the way.

When floating, give wade fishers a wide berth. Leave them plenty of extra water to fish by not casting into it. This helps create the illusion that they have some water to fish that hasn't already been flogged by a parade of boats on busier days. To a

This boat is floating behind wade fishers so as not to interfere with their fishing. Communication and consideration are key in avoiding river conflicts. On big rivers, stay far away from waders. On little rivers, ask them the best way for you to go around, so you do not scare their trout.

wading angler, boats look closer than floaters realize. If the other side of the river is unoccupied, row over there as soon as a wade fisher comes into view. Resist the urge to make one more cast to a hot spot just upstream from him.

Space yourself evenly from other boats. Slow down to fall farther behind. If you're ahead, float a little faster for a while to put some space between you and a boat that's right behind you. Don't get into racing matches to be first to hot spots. If you're going to do that, why not just get a big power boat and rip the river up getting there? While you're at it, take a seine net and get all the fish. There seem to be a lot of people, including some guides, on the river these days who would be better off on a tennis court or playing some other urban and concrete-based competition sport. Go with the flow, fish where you are, forget the rest of humanity, and enjoy the day. That's what a day on the river is for.

When floating rivers, be aware of different states' trespass regulations. Some states allow access to the bank and streambed below the high-water mark. In other states, the landowner owns the banks and streambed, and even anchoring is technically illegal. Future floating rights could depend on how well today's float anglers observe (or change) current laws. Though it shouldn't have to be mentioned, don't trespass or litter on stream. Pick up other people's litter when it's convenient, and take it out in your boat. When everybody does a little to clean up the river environment, the results start showing in short order. Courtesy, respect for landowner rights, giving wade fishers plenty of room, and spacing evenly from other fishing boats are all daily etiquette requirements when float-fishing rivers.

NEGOTIATING RAMPS

Watching a novice back a trailer down a tight ramp is always amusing, unless you're in a hurry to get on or off the river and are right behind him. He probably won't grasp the basic trailering concept without experience or instruction.

Backing is the trickiest part of trailering. It feels unnatural on the first attempts. To turn the trailer one way when backing, you have to turn the vehicle the opposite way. When, or actually just before, the trailer has turned enough, straighten the vehicle to push the trailer backward. Because most drift-boat trailers have short wheelbases and tongues, they turn quickly—perhaps a little too quickly for a beginner—for they seem to want to turn one way or the other even when you don't want them to. Indeed, going straight back and keeping the trailer backing in a straight line is the hardest thing to do. Only experience with a particular rig and trailer will give you the necessary feel for the

When rigging up or tearing down, do it away from the ramp, especially if others are waiting to use it. If the ramp is empty, dump your boat in, park your vehicle, and do your rigging at anchor.

job. It's easier to learn on big spacious ramps than on narrow, steep, angled ones.

Practice using your mirrors right from the start to follow your trailer's backward progress. This is much easier than straining your neck to look over your shoulders. You'll want mirrors on both sides of your vehicle. When the trailer begins turning even a little too much to one side, immediately correct by turning the vehicle in the opposite direction. Don't allow the trailer to get way off track or jackknife, because this can damage the trailer or vehicle. Slow and easy is the way to learn. You'll be more likely to oversteer than anything, and to let the trailer turn too far off-course before correcting its path. In a tight situation, you can unhitch the trailer and manually align it with the ramp as long as the ground is level. Rehitch it before heading down a steep ramp. Some people put a hitch on their front bumper. Hooking the boat there makes it easier to maneuver down difficult ramps. A couple of people can usually drag a loaded boat trailer to one side or the other, helping a beginner along.

It's easy enough to see your boat and trailer when you are backing at the put-in. A boatless trailer at the take-out (and possibly in the dark) is another matter. It can be impossible to see a narrow, boatless trailer when backing with a tall vehicle, which blocks your low view. The trailer comes into sight only when it's swinging to one side, which at times means it's turned farther than you want it to. With a pickup truck, you can drop the tailgate to see the trailer, but this isn't always an option with some other vehicles.

There are ways to work around this. For starters, you can have a boatmate behind your vehicle giving hand signals and possibly using a flashlight to point and illuminate the way. You could also attach tall wands (with or without small flags) to the outside edges of your trailer near the back end. These should be tall enough and angled outward so as to be seen in your mirrors when you are backing straight. They can be permanent or removable. It helps to have widely placed mirrors on both sides of your vehicle, such as those used by RVers. This provides a little more mirror angle to help you see behind your rig. Oh, by the way, never trust somebody who is backing up. Keep your eyes open and be ready to move!

When you buy a trailer, try to get one that's wide enough to see from both mirrors when car and trailer are aligned. This will make it easier for you to see as you back, and you can also see both trailer tires when you are driving in order to check for flat tires or burned-up bearings (a wobbling wheel). Backing your hubs in and out of water can ruin them quickly if you don't stay on top of the regreasing game. I try not to get my trailer axle hubs in the water at all.

The end result—beautiful fish in a beautiful setting. To some, float fishing is more than a pastime, it's a way of life.

My trailer is a little wider and longer than average, because I have a motorcycle rack built on the tongue. I can see the trailer in both mirrors when it is straight, and it backs well, having a longer wheelbase. It's a little tougher to back down very angled, twisty ramps, but that is rarely a problem in my case. I like being able to see both trailer tires when I drive.

When heading down the road with a trailer, you'll need to take corners a little wider than usual. Watch the trailer's cornering progress in the mirror. Soon you'll get over jumping curbs with the trailer tire, scraping your boat on ramp-edge bushes, or possibly doing more serious damage to it. Most drift-boat trailers are short enough to follow a vehicle well; you can drive in a near-normal cornering fashion.

Backing trailers takes the ability to conceptualize and lots of practice to master, kind of like rowing. It's just one more skill that will grow out of your float-fishing experiences.

Index